'Like me, you will think, *If this gentleman can, by the grace of God, overcome his limitations, I can, too.*'
JONI EARECKSON TADA

'Have you ever felt like giving up? Then this is the book for you. Brian's love for life is infectious; his determination not to allow his physical disability to make him an outcast or socially isolated is awesome and inspirational; his love for Jesus Christ and selfless desire to serve those who suffer in hopelessness is challenging and uplifting.

'This is a story that will encourage thousands of lives. It has already encouraged me.'
SARAH DE CARVALHO

'I was deeply moved, when I first met Brian eight years ago, by witnessing first-hand the courageous way he has put his life into words. The story will continually move you from laughter to tears and then straight back to laughter again. I defy anyone not to be touched by this man and what he has to say.

Whilst each one of us should hang our heads in shame as to the cause of Brian's disability, we should all be equally as proud and thankful for what God had done for him in his incredible life, and he for our incredible God.
RICK WAKEMAN

To

Hereward College

Look, No Hands!

The Inspiring Story of
Brian Gault

with Helena Rogers

Blessings

Brian x

Hodder & Stoughton
LONDON SYDNEY AUCKLAND

10th February 2004

Unless otherwise indicated, Scripture quotations are taken from the
HOLY BIBLE, NEW INTERNATIONAL VERSION.
Copyright © 1973, 1978, 1984 by International Bible Society.
Used by permission. All rights reserved.

Permission to quote from the following sources is gratefully
acknowledged: on p. 86, Gloria and William Gaither,
'Because He Lives', copyright © 1971 Gaither Music Company/
WJG Inc/Kingsway's Thankyou Music. Used by permission; on
p. 141, Graham Kendrick, 'Meekness and Majesty', copyright ©
1986 Kingsway's Thankyou Music, PO Box 75, Eastbourne,
East Sussex, BN23 6NW. Used by Permission.

British Library Cataloguing in Publication Data
A record for this book is available from the British Library

ISBN 0 340 74636 X

Typeset by Avon Dataset Ltd, Bidford-on-Avon, Warks

Printed and bound in Great Britain by
Clays Ltd, St Ives plc

The paper and board used in this paperback are natural recyclable
products made from wood grown in sustainable forests.
The manufacturing processes conform to the environmental
regulations of the country of origin.

Hodder & Stoughton
A Division of Hodder Headine Ltd
338 Euston Road
London NW1 3BH
www.madaboutbooks.com

This book is dedicated, for every reason,
to MY MOTHER

Contents

Before you begin . . .

I've gotten used to being on display. Whether it's the child studying my wheelchair, the senior citizen across the way smiling sympathetically, or the waiter eyeing me carefully as I use my bent spoon to eat pieces of hamburger, I'm aware that people are watching. Some might watch out of pity, some out of admiration. All watch, I sense, with unspoken questions.

It's part of the territory that comes with a disability.

It's what Brian Gault faces every day. But like Brian, I choose to think that people's unspoken questions are, for the most part, good-natured. That's because Brian and I, as followers of Jesus Christ, are constrained to think the best of others. We are called to be on display (as any Christian is). We are encouraged by God's Word to smile from the inside-out as the strength of God shows up bountifully through our physical limitations. When people eye Brian, using his feet as 'hands', I believe they are thinking, *How great his God must be to inspire such faith and confidence*.

Somehow, I don't think Brian minds being on display. Brian's story inspires faith and confidence in people who observe him. People who become his friend. Including me. I remember the first time I met Brian, I was struck by his warm smile, sunlit confidence in Christ, and his genuine way of reaching out to others and involving them in the fold of fellowship. To be honest, I hardly noticed the fact that he had no arms! His happy-hearted disposition bolsters me greatly.

Brian's entire life showcases 1 Corinthians 12:24–6 where we learn that, 'God has combined the members of the body and has given great honour to the parts that lacked it, so that there should be no division in the body, but that its parts should have equal concern for each other. If one part suffers, every part suffers with it; if one part is honoured, every part rejoices with it.'

The man whose autobiography you hold in your hands may be lacking literal 'members of his body', but God has blessed him with the great honour of encouraging and strengthening the rest of the body of Christ. How ironic that God should use a man who has no hands to move the rest of us to reach out and touch and embrace others. Truly, God has strengthened the Church through the powerful and poignant example of Brian Gault.

This is what will strike you about *Look, No Hands!* From the first chapter to the last, your heart will be warmed as you read how Brian has dealt with his limitations. You will learn of a man whose soul is settled and whose peace is profound. You will discover someone who leads, not with parade and noise, but by influence. And like me, you will think, *If this gentleman can, by the grace of God, overcome his limitations, I can, too.*

Joni Eareckson Tada
Through the Roof
Summer 1999

Acknowledgments

I am indebted to many friends who helped bring about this book:

To those family members and friends throughout the British Isles who made valuable inputs at different times, playing such significant parts in fashioning and moulding my life, I say a sincere thank you.

To Ted Hall and Keith Markham for their advice and support, and for continually e-mailing messages and information to Helena.

To my work colleagues for allowing me to have nine months off to write my story.

Finally, to Helena Rogers for patiently and courageously pulling all my thoughts and emotions together.

Prologue

I sat looking at the television with tears streaming down my face. A little girl, five or six years old, stood barefoot in a muddy pool of water with the dilapidated shack of her shantytown home forlornly behind her. A vacant, hopeless expression matched the dejected stance of her emaciated little body – and she had no arms.

The commentator revealed that the child had been affected by the drug thalidomide that had been prescribed to her mother during the first three months of pregnancy, to counteract the side effects of drugs for leprosy.

But this was not a report of something that happened thirty years ago. It was happening even as I watched – in 1993!

I could not believe my eyes! Surely, I thought, thalidomide had been consigned to the dustbin as soon as its devastating effects became clear. Over the few years of its use in the late 1950s and early 1960s, many children throughout the world had been born without some or all limbs because their mothers had been prescribed thalidomide during pregnancy. But I had assumed that I must have been one of its last victims. Here, however, a television programme set out to show that far from discarding thalidomide, it remained in use – mainly in the Third World where leprosy still exists.

The programme I watched majored on the country of Brazil where half a million people are affected by leprosy, many of them poor and uneducated. Often they are not warned that thalidomide causes harm to unborn babies, and any printed warning goes unheeded by those who cannot read. Even worse – thalidomide can be obtained over the counter with no questions asked!

Together with the programme makers, I asked the questions: Why? How? Have we not learnt from the experiences of thirty years ago?

Here in the British Isles, despite the long wrangles with the drug company, all thalidomides received good health care and education, culminating finally with compensation for their loss. But what could children in Brazil expect? The little girl that touched my heart had no future beyond that of poverty and hopelessness.

And yet thalidomide is still prescribed and used. Its efficacy in some branches of medicine is undoubted, but the dangers should be made clear. Children continue to be born limbless. How long will it be before someone takes the initiative to make the situation clear to those who need to know and halt the misery that can be caused?

I cannot halt the tide alone, but the proceeds of this book will all go to help support the maimed thalidomide children of Brazil.

1

Born unique

My arms were my handicap. I struggled with them, fought them, *tried* to use them but when, at last, everyone gave up *making* me use them, I began to really live. To most people, the smart, plastic, artificial arms strapped to my chest and manipulated with an attached canister of oxygen gas were a wonder of technology. To me they were cumbersome, painful and embarrassing, and they restricted my ease of action at every turn.

From babyhood I had been able to use my toes perfectly well for almost any task – to take a bottle, play with my rattle and, as I grew, to eat, write, draw and play. I had no need of artificial arms hanging from my shoulders – I could manage far more easily with my nimble toes. The hated arms certainly made it less embarrassing for my mother to present me to a pitying public, but they caused *me* untold anguish, anger and frustration.

At my birth, my parents were offered several alternatives regarding my upbringing – none of them the option of keeping me and raising me at home. Institutionalisation was deemed suitable for a child born without arms – or perhaps adoption, although why adoptive parents were thought able to manage better than real parents is a mystery – but the thought that my parents might love me and want to keep me did not enter the equation.

My mother had instinctively realised that this pregnancy did not seem the same as her other pregnancies. She said that she 'felt different'. She could not put it into words, but she knew 'something did not feel quite right'. Then, when the baby arrived at 2.30 a.m. on 23 September 1961 after a long and painful labour, he was not met with joyful cries of 'It's a boy!' but with a strained silence, and the order to 'roll him in a towel and take him to another room . . .'

She had to recover sufficiently before she could be told that her new baby had no arms. Even so, the news rent her heart in two. 'How can I see this little baby with no arms?' she wept. And then inevitably cried, 'Why? Why has this happened to us? Is God punishing us for something?'

Her cousin, a doctor, visiting to console my mother, tried to reassure her. 'Don't think like that, Isobel,' she begged. 'You are the fifth woman in recent months to have a child born with missing limbs. It has nothing to do with punishment.'

The fifth? *Five* children in recent months . . .? At first my mother felt relief that she did not grieve alone, but anger quickly replaced the grief. If five children had been born with defects, then something must be causing it. What was going on?

Two months later, on 27 November 1961, the drug thalidomide, prescribed as a sedative to help relieve morning sickness in pregnancy, was withdrawn from sale. No one knows the full extent of the damage to human lives that thalidomide caused during the three and a half years of its availability on the market, but it is estimated that over 450 maimed children survive in Britain, with up to 10,000 in other countries worldwide. The

United States, however, did not suffer extensively from the tragedy. Dr Frances Kelsey, a pharmacologist and physician who bore the responsibility of releasing thalidomide for use in America, became suspicious during trials when six babies were born with deformities. She therefore delayed giving her approval to release the drug for so long that it was withdrawn before it could do more harm.

Research later discovered that thalidomide affected the foetus in the first three months of pregnancy, when the child's limbs were forming. The deformities included the absence of arms, sometimes with flipper-like appendages at the shoulder instead, or no legs, just toes from the hips, or even a completely limbless body leaving a trunk and head only.

In 1958, thalidomide was hailed as a wonder drug. It was advertised as 'completely safe, and an answer to the mounting deaths due to barbiturate poisoning'. Then in the increasing euphoria, it was recommended also for use in psychiatry, geriatrics, neurology, dermatology, paediatrics and obstetrics, and advertising stated that 'thalidomide can be given with complete safety to pregnant women and nursing mothers without adverse effects on mother or child' (Distillers Company [Biochemicals] Limited, 1961). By the end of March 1961, nearly sixty-four million tablets had been sold, and April turned out to be the best month yet for sales in the three years of its launch.

As alarm began to spread with the increasing rumours of problems with the drug, the makers, Grunenthal of Germany, frantically tried to defend their commercially-successful invention. They appeared to be convinced of its efficacy and blind to the increasing number of frightening reports coming in from all parts of the world. By November 1961, however, public opinion left them no choice but to withdraw the drug.

It was to be some time after my birth that my parents

discovered the reason for my deformities. My father had taken the news badly from the start. He had no idea how to cope with such a situation, and therefore immersed himself in his work and with the animals on the smallholding where we lived in Ballyclare, Northern Ireland.

My mother determined to care for me at home in spite of the staff's intention to keep me in hospital longer than the four weeks I had been there since my birth. She was dissatisfied with the level of care I received, and insisted that I be taken home. The hospital staff probably did not give much opposition to the plan because apparently I cried incessantly!

Once home, her task began in earnest. With an older stepson, Derek, and two young children already – my brother, Alan, then aged five, and sister, Patricia, two – she now had to contend with a new baby who had been born disabled. The initial shock of giving birth to such a baby had been immense, but to discover that the tragedy was not a one-in-a-million chance, but the result of a drug that she had been prescribed, heaped added burdens of illogical guilt upon her. With her sensitive nature and timid personality, it is not surprising that she suffered a nervous breakdown. She recovered quickly, but learning to cope with her little child took longer.

It proved very difficult at first for her to face others. She herself knew the confusion of not knowing what to say when confronted by disability, so her instinct was to protect herself, her visitor and me from the embarrassed looks which she anticipated she would get. She could not bear to risk the looks of horror on the faces of potential admirers as they stared into the pram, so she would wrap me in a shawl and walk me round the house for fresh air. The hens and the pigs never passed comment or showed signs of surprise. It was safe with them. But if anyone called unexpectedly, she would grab me and rush into the kitchen out of the way.

And so it might have gone on – if a friend had not caught her by surprise as she walked down the lane one day. The genuine love and empathy she received from that dear friend was enough to break the ice. From then on, Lily, her friend and warden of the local church, would spend a lot of time helping Mum to come to terms with what had happened.

'It's no accident that your Brian has no arms,' she would insist confidently as she bounced me on her knee. 'God has a purpose for him – you wait and see!'

Something else also helped my mother to come into the open with her tragedy. Living in a rural area, it sometimes became necessary to call out the vet for one of the animals. To this end, therefore, we had a telephone installed. Being the only one in the area at the time, the word soon got around, and before long the neighbouring farmers or their wives found it much easier to call the vet by coming over to our house.

Soon everyone knew about me, or had seen me, and the secret could be kept no longer. Mum discovered that she did not receive looks of horror or glances of embarrassment – just offers of help and genuine love for her little baby. This made it easier for my mother to accept the situation, but she was still tormented by fears about how I would manage as I grew up. It would be fine while she was near to take care of me, but what about the future? What quality of life would a grown man have who had to be fed, dressed and helped to do any everyday task? For surely the lack of arms would prevent him from any kind of normal life.

The pastor from the large Ballylinney Presbyterian Church just down the road became a regular visitor. The Rev. Young became a source of strength and encouragement as he popped in from time to time, but he wondered why they had not suggested having their little boy christened. Mum seemed rather non-committal about the prospect, not wishing to make a public show of her baby's disabilities, but the pastor went on: 'We could have the ceremony during the morning service . . .'

My mother flinched. There would be so many people at the service.

'Or in the afternoon – it's quieter then,' he persisted, and then with inspiration, 'What about having it here at home? There is no rule that says it must be in the church. We are simply offering this little boy to God – and God will hear wherever we are.'

My mother gave in. The christening was arranged, and on 12 April 1962, I became a member of the Church in a little ceremony in our living-room.

I soon began to demonstrate that I was far from helpless. Any doubts about how I would manage to play with my toys or hold my teething ring with no arms were soon dispelled. I had two perfectly good feet with five very active toes on each foot – so I simply used those instead! It was all so natural. When a biscuit came towards me in my pram, my foot reached up to take it with my toes. When a friendly face waved something interesting at me, my legs jumped up to hold it.

My feet and legs developed the grasping action in the same way that arms and hands in any other baby would respond. And when I lay down to go to sleep, my teddy bear nestled snugly between my legs.

Before long, lack of arms was no barrier to my doing most things. I increasingly got into mischief, and my mother found she had to watch me just as she had watched my brother and sister. The heavy poker lying in the hearth was a favourite target as I learned to crawl. I would bump along on my behind and reach out for that interesting poker with my feet. Many a time Mum would find me with the poker in my mouth and blackened all over! Once again she would have to wash away the coal dust from my mouth, ears, nose and feet. Then the poker would be moved out of my reach until someone forgot and put it down on the hearth again, and then I would seize my chance for another game.

'Oh, how you loved that poker,' my mother told me in later years. 'You were impossible to keep clean!'

The continual bumping along played havoc with my trousers. It seems hard to believe, but Mum insists that I wore a pair out nearly every week! She patched and mended, mended and patched, but found herself having to make numerous new pairs from every conceivable piece of spare strong material she could find! Nothing was wasted. Old coats or suits – anything strong became another pair of trousers for me to wear out in record time!

In the minds of most people, disability equals weakness. This, of course, is not necessarily true, and I demonstrated the futility of the notion by my persistent determination. I did not lie passive in my cot. I pulled myself up at every opportunity – strengthening my back and leg muscles in the process – in order not to miss anything that went on. My mother glowed with pride when I sat up earlier than either of my two siblings, and optimism began to replace despair.

Insatiable curiosity led me to find ways of solving any problem. The only difference between other babies and me lay in the fact that instead of using hands, I used toes. Mum began to test my inventive instincts. She offered me a sweet wrapped in paper, and I simply unwrapped it with my toes – taking it with my *left* foot, she noticed. But even then, it was not easy for her to stand by and watch me struggle. It would be so much easier to help or do the task for me. She had been advised, however, that my independence lay in achieving for myself, and although often anguished at my exertion she tried to steel herself to let me continue until successful.

My first steps were awaited eagerly. They came during one of our family holidays in Portrush, on the northern coast of Northern Ireland. For many years in succession we caught the train at Ballyclare and travelled the seventy miles along the coast to where we would hire a caravan for a fortnight. It was a wonderful time when we could all be together in a relaxed atmosphere, and we looked forward to these times avidly.

The long, golden sands of the beaches were paradise for us as children. I particularly loved the feel of the sand, although I insisted on eating a lot of it! I knew all about sand from my sandpit at home where I would play as my father fed the chickens and the pigs, and although I liked the gritty softness between my toes, I would often lean down to feel it with my face. My despairing mother would find me with sand in my hair, nose, eyes, ears and mouth! Who knew how much I had consumed? And what would it do to my digestive system? She had visions of all kinds of horrors, but for all that, I did not seem to come to much harm. On the beach, however, where she could watch me and relax at the same time, I could not fall and hurt myself, and I could play happily for a long time before we all trooped back to the caravan for tea.

It did not take me long to discover that the u-shaped seating revealed after the beds had been put away gave me a long, uninterrupted *soft* surface on which to crawl. But if I stretched upwards and took a step . . . down I fell – but came to no harm on the cushions. My parents laughed and clapped! My sister and brother came to look and joined in the praise as I repeated the feat. Soon the visitors in the neighbouring caravans were brought in to watch my amazing achievements as I added more and more steps to please the assembled company.

'Oh, what a show-off you were!' laughed my mother proudly. 'You added more steps each day!'

Holidays also meant 'ice cream'. There were no shops selling ice cream near where we lived, and mobile shops did not reach our country smallholding. So one of the first things we children always wanted as soon as we arrived in Portrush was – ice cream! Unfortunately I tried so hard to make sure I didn't drop my ice cream that I would squeeze it too hard between my toes. This meant that the bottom of the cone would begin to disintegrate and soon I would be drenched in white, sticky liquid! This, and the warm weather which melted the ice cream much too fast for my baby mouth to consume, meant that I lost more between my toes and down my legs than I ate!

On the whole I had no problem with eating – to my mind. I grasped a spoon between my toes as well as any child with fingers. But eating with a spoon was not the quickest method. I often used to watch the pigs outside in the sty. They had no hands either, but they soon demolished their trough full of food with snouts deeply buried in the soggy mess. Then there was Laddie, our dog. He would do the same. His long tongue would leave his dish pristine clean. *And* they didn't get food spread all down their fronts! It seemed a much more sensible way to eat.

So I, too, often used the method that came most naturally – I simply ducked my head into the dish and slurped away! Sausages, chips, baked beans – all went the same way – and much faster than my brother and sister could manage with their knives and forks! 'It's not fair!' they would complain. 'Why should Brian be allowed to eat like that when we aren't?'

It was indeed unfair, I am sure, but so long as we had no company, my mother allowed me this indulgence. When visitors called, however, it was different. I could exhibit my dexterity with a fork and spoon. Everyone used to think me so clever, and I revelled in the praise, but as far as I was concerned I only did what the others did – but with toes instead of fingers. What could be strange about that?

Although I learned to lift a cup with my toes, the hospital supplied us with long lengths of tubular plastic to be used like straws with hot drinks. I tried, but often bits of vegetable would get stuck in the tubes, and no matter what I did, I could not shift it. Then there was the added hazard of tasting washing-up liquid with the first mouthful of a clean straw. I much preferred to use a cup, but wait for it to cool enough to hold with my feet.

My parents realised the need to strengthen my toes, and sought advice from the hospital. The physiotherapist suggested that I should have sets of Lego bricks and plasticine. With these I could develop strength and dexterity by picking up the small bricks and forming buildings, towers and toys, and with the plasticine I would mould toy cars, buses, tractors and farmyard animals. I could grip with my toes as well as any hand with fingers. The fascinating toys provided me with hours of pleasure.

Our doctor also recommended that my mother take me to join with other thalidomide children at a special day nursery at the city hospital. Mum was so anxious to do everything possible to help me that she did her best to comply with the recommendation, even though she was four months' pregnant with my sister Gwen at the time. We had no car in those days, so the journey to the hospital meant that my sister Pat and I had to walk with Mum for twenty-five minutes just to get to the nearest bus stop.

Then when we reached Belfast, we all had to walk for another forty-five minutes before we could reach our destination! It was a routine we kept up for several weeks before someone noticed that we were exhausted before we even got there! For the following nine months, friends arranged daily transport for us, and finally an ambulance solved all our travel problems by collecting and returning us each day.

I loved to be with other children and the nursery offered wonderful opportunities for play. At first they taught me exercises which would strengthen my legs, feet and toes. I liked the new games and would come home to demonstrate them to my brother and sisters. How we laughed as they tried to copy my antics. Then I would follow them and join in their games.

My mother watched as I pitted my wits against my 'complete' brothers and sisters. She loved to see me enjoying myself, but would this be sufficient to provide me with a future? How would I cope at school? How could I earn a living? The workplace was competitive enough at the best of times. How would a man with no arms cope in the relentless rat race of everyday work? Was there something that could be done to enhance my chances . . .?

2

Not good enough

I had not long passed my second birthday when I discovered we were going on an aeroplane to get 'my arms'. My mother seemed quite excited about this venture, but I could not see what the fuss was about. Why did I need to get 'arms'? My legs and toes were perfectly capable of doing all I needed, so why should I have to have 'arms'? I did look forward to going up into the sky in the kind of plane I had seen in my picture books, but 'arms' were certainly no cause for excitement.

As the day drew near, my father seemed quieter than usual but my mother, who was by now six months' pregnant with my sister Gwen, hurried about getting our cases packed, and trying at the same time to instil a little enthusiasm for the trip.

'I can't see why this is necessary,' my father would say, thinking of my mother and her last two pregnancies – the one before mine which resulted in a dangerous miscarriage, and my own birth which proved to be a very difficult labour. 'He manages quite well with his toes,' he reasoned. 'Why do we need to go to all this trouble?'

'Look,' my mother would patiently reply, 'we have to give him this chance. Otherwise when he grows up and sees his friends with arms, he might wonder why we didn't give him the same opportunity.'

Dad had no choice but to agree, and before long I found myself climbing into the little plane which would take us from Aldergrove, Belfast, to Edinburgh, Scotland. It was only a seventy-minute flight, but I did not enjoy it after all. I liked the long climb upwards as I watched the familiar town and countryside retreat to become a panorama of toys, but the higher we got, the more effect the air pressure had on my eardrums and the more uncomfortable I began to feel. I had always been susceptible to ear problems, and this experience did them no good at all.

I could sense the unease of both my parents when we arrived at the Princess Margaret Rose Hospital in Edinburgh. This was the northern centre of prosthetic limb development, where all those living roughly north of Birmingham came to be fitted with artificial arms or legs. Those south of Birmingham would be directed to the centre at Roehampton. Development of artificial limbs had been going on for some years, but as the thalidomide tragedy began to unfold, experimentation increased.

Had I known what lay ahead of me, I might have been more frightened. I did not know then that this was the place where I, and many others like me, would be fitted with a substitute limb or limbs, and which would necessitate having to spend a lot of time away from our homes being trained to use what my father had described as 'contraptions'.

The unofficial line was that we were being 'rebuilt'. Public outrage and guilt that such a disaster had occurred caused an upsurge of desire to do everything possible to give back to the young victims what they had been denied, but the road to 'rebuilding' was a very long and hard one.

The exterior of the hospital building loomed ominously as we made our way to the clinic. It gave no indication of the beautiful wooded grounds of conifer trees to the rear where in later years I would gain a little light relief as I romped and played with other children during respites in our training.

The clinic lay a little behind the main building in chalet-like accommodation. It housed a large functional room, a lounge, kitchen, bathroom and at least four bedrooms with multi-sleeping facilities. All the furniture and apparatus had been custom-built for use with wheelchairs and children with missing limbs.

We had already met Dr David Simpson in Belfast some time before. He came to demonstrate to parents of limbless children the kind of artificial limbs that had been developed with thalidomide victims very much in mind. He told my parents that he had 'upper limb prostheses' which would be ideal for me, and which would bring many benefits to improve my quality of life.

My father was sceptical. He could see how naturally I used my toes, feet and legs. Dr Simpson tried to convince him of the advantages to be gained.

'Think about it,' he persuaded, 'it may be all right now, but what about when Brian grows up? He may be self-conscious in public places when everyone around him has arms. What will it be like for him in cafés, on buses and at work? He will need self-confidence, and you know how difficult it is for a child if he is different from his friends . . .'

My father did not seem convinced yet. Brian seemed completely self-confident already, and even proud of the way he managed everything just as well as any other child.

'But what will happen if you don't give him the chance to try arms? Will he thank you for denying him this wonderful opportunity? And besides, all the other thalidomide children are having them. Brian wouldn't want to be left out, would he?'

Bearing in mind the enormous amount of money that had been sunk into prosthesis development, it was probably not surprising that Dr Simpson felt obliged to press the benefits of technology on sceptical parents.

My mother did not take much convincing that I should be given the chance to try these wonderful inventions, but my father only gave in after much persuasion. Doubts about the enterprise remained with him, however.

Everything was new and strange to me in the clinic: the special furniture, bustling medical staff and odd-looking equipment. I did find it interesting to meet other children like myself, but when I was shown a bed with a cupboard where my mother began storing my belongings, I began to fear. Where were my parents going to sleep? And if we had to stay here, what would happen to Laddie, my dog? He was my constant companion. What would he do if I weren't there with him?

My mother's obvious distress increased my anxiety, and when they gently told me that I would have to remain here in this strange place alone, while the doctors showed me how to use the 'arms', I was terrified. I leaned close to my mother, trying to wrap my legs around her to keep her near, and looked appealingly at my father to rescue me. Surely they would not abandon me to the unknown care of strangers?

It was no good, however. In no time, it seemed to me, I found myself torn from my mother's grasp and forced to watch her and my father retreat, leaving me defenceless. I could not believe that my mother would do such a thing. She had always been so close to me. Now, at my hour of deepest need, she had simply walked out and left me. I was inconsolable.

I may have eventually stopped crying, but the hurt remained.

I had to submit to the authority of the staff – who tried their best to cheer me up, but deep within I blamed my mother for cruelly abandoning me.

The full realisation as to what was going to happen soon dawned. I saw other children struggling to use strange, stiff arms and legs, and realised that I had been brought here to do the same. This is what had been meant when they told me I would have 'new arms'. Suddenly it all fell into place, but it did not ease my hurt – it added to it. Why did my mother feel that I needed arms? Didn't she love me as I was? Did I have to look like other children before my family would take me home again? I had thought I was special to them, but it seemed they wanted me to look like everyone else.

I was desperately unhappy as the staff put me to bed that night. I lay in the stiff, white sheets and thought about home. I imagined Laddie walking through the house with his tail down searching for me. He would eventually lie down on his blanket as unhappily as I would. I eventually fell asleep from exhaustion.

I awoke to a strange new world of sounds and people. It all went to reinforce my feeling of rejection and alienation from home. I allowed myself to be washed and dressed, and then, with all the other children, led into breakfast.

The first step to 'arms' began with having a plaster cast made of the whole of my upper body. The smiling nurses did little to lessen my feelings of abandonment, and I felt the oozing bandages of liquid plaster wrapping around me like a prisoner's chains. The feelings of fear increased as the plaster set, encasing me in a hard shell. But this was nothing compared to my terror when they brought out large electric clippers to cut me out of the shell. I had no mother to turn to, to protect me from danger. She had left me to the mercy of my captors.

The next ten weeks were a nightmare. All the weekdays were

spent at the clinic, but as it closed for the weekends, each Friday evening we were shunted into the children's ward in the hospital where we stayed until Monday morning. The nurses and doctors who tried to encourage me with the lure of 'new arms which will help you do all sorts of new things like all the other boys and girls' became simply tormentors who forcibly kept me from my family and from Laddie. Getting back to my home became an all-important end that I longed for with all my being.

For some time after the plaster cast had been made, nothing happened. I did not understand that the technicians were making artificial arms specifically moulded to match the cast of my body. The process was a very complicated one. Artificial arms consisted of many parts: first a bulky harness which fitted onto the shoulders; then straps and hooks fastened around the chest and waist to keep everything in place; shoulder pressure pads containing electric contacts which provided the movement for working the arms; a power pack consisting of a gas cylinder attached to the back of the harness; and then the arms themselves: heavy metal rods and tubes filled with wires, connectors, bolts, and all kinds of electronic paraphernalia to make them work, and with a gripping mechanism or a hook where the hand should be. It all meant hours of painstaking work putting the parts together and making many minute adjustments to each prosthesis so that it would fit the specifically moulded casing.

When the time came for my first fitting, my worst fears were realised. As they strapped the hard casing around my body, I felt trapped. I looked at the ugly contraptions hanging rigidly from my shoulders. They looked nothing like real arms. Their weight combined with the restriction of the body casing increased a feeling of being shackled, and added to all this, I felt an acute humiliation that I had not been acceptable up until now. I apparently needed all this equipment to make me presentable to the world. Even my parents had abandoned me until I could reach an approved standard. My toes had been quite sufficient for all my needs, but now I had to give up all that and learn to do things in a completely different way. Why did everyone think it was wrong for me to use my toes? Was it wrong to be different from everyone else? If I had to resemble 'normal people' before I could go home, why didn't they give me proper arms and not these hideous, heavy, uncomfortable monstrosities?

Of course, at just two and a half years old, I could not put all my fears into words. I could only show my confusion by crying, shouting and refusing to be forced into complying. As I flung myself into yet another tantrum of frustration, the nurses' smiling faces changed into frowns. 'Stop being silly,' they would say. 'If you try hard, you will be able to do all sorts of things with your new arms. Don't you want to be like the other boys and girls?'

No, I didn't want to be like all the others. I wanted to be myself. And anyway, I could do with my toes almost everything everyone else could do with their fingers. Why did I have to learn to do it all another way?

My captors were, of course, stronger than me, and they always won. Every day I was forced into donning the cold metal casing and the heavy arms.

I could hardly stand when the full equipment had been fitted. It altered my balance and I had to learn to stand upright. I fell often at first, and having no way of putting out my arms to save myself, I usually fell on my face. Even if I fell another way, it would force the edges of the body casing into my flesh. I became used to the sight of black bruising or red, angry marks on my face and body. It made it all the more painful when I had to put the casing on the next time.

In addition was the chafing where the harness cut into my shoulders and back. And all this was not so that I would be able to do all the things other children do – because I could already do them! It seemed to me to be entirely so that I would look like everyone else!

My instruction began in earnest. I had to learn to cope first with the heavy weight on my shoulders, then how to move so that the pressure pads would react on the arms. Flexing shoulder muscles in a particular way made the arms move up, down or sideways and then a strap around my chest controlled the opening and closing mechanism of the right hook. I had to expand my chest to make the hook open. All this was supposed to make it easier for me to hold a spoon, to draw or to play with my toys.

It took a great deal of concentration to make the arms do what they were supposed to do and, for a little boy of two and a half who did not even possess the will to make the experiment work, it was an almost unendurable burden.

I would be staring at my lunch of sausage, chips and beans and longing to throw off the heavy weight of arms so that I could get at the food with a spoon in my toes, but I had to try and make the arms do all that. With a great deal of effort I would manage to pick up the spoon after several attempts, and then set my mind to getting food on the spoon and the spoon to my mouth. I did manage it eventually, but often, no sooner had I taken a mouthful when the arms seemed to take on a life of their own and would swing upwards, sending the food in an arc over my head to land on an unsuspecting child at another table! My frustration knew no bounds. If only they would let me get on with my food in my own way. I could eat it in no time without having to struggle until it got cold.

As the technology was still in its infancy, the mechanism often went wrong. A wire could easily become loose or a pressure pad jam, and it might take an hour or so for the problem to be put right. As young as I was, I fumed inside. I could not justify the stupidity of the whole process.

Another hazard came with the gas cylinder. In the first place, every movement I made would be accompanied by a hissing noise as the pressure pad contacts caused the propellant gas to be released and the arms to move. As I grew up, I found this – and not the fact of having no natural arms – acutely embarrassing when I was with 'normal' people. These uncomfortable, cumbersome weights were supposed to make me more presentable to others. Instead they hissed and creaked every time I made the slightest movement – that is, while there still happened to be gas in the cylinder. Sooner or later it naturally ran out, and no matter what I happened to be doing at the time – writing, playing or even holding a cup of lemonade – without warning the arms would revert to 'crucify' position – sticking out sideways – and I would be left looking foolish and helpless until the empty cylinder was replaced. Oh, how infuriating they were!

The daily programme of training became one long trial which I found harder and harder to cope with. I had previously been a carefree, happy-go-lucky child, with a constant smile and determination to do anything anyone else could do. Now, separated from all I held dear and submitted to the futility of trying to become 'normal', I changed to an angry, frustrated little boy who had frequent temper tantrums.

Then one day I was told that I could go home. My parents were coming to fetch me. But once again I felt torn in two. One half of me thrilled at the thought of seeing my home and family again, and especially to be reunited with Laddie, the dog, but the other half of me agonised that my parents could ever have abandoned me here at all.

The resulting meeting with my mother proved completely different from her excited expectations. As she and my father came into view, I had eyes only for Dad. I ran to him and flung myself into his arms, but Mum might as well not have been there. I could not look at her. Although I knew deep within that both my parents had ultimately been responsible for my assumed rejection, it seemed to be my mother who received the brunt of my anguish. Somehow I could not forgive her. She had been my constant help and companion; I relied on her to encourage me and care for me, but she let me down badly. She had abandoned me at my most vulnerable moment. Mum offered the sweets that she had brought for me, but I could not accept them. I turned away from her as she had turned away from me.

I could not know then that my mother had suffered in leaving me just as much as I suffered through being left. She had anguished over her happy little boy who had to be torn from his loving home to be cared for by strangers. When he was born she had never even considered giving him up to institutional care – an option she knew had been offered to other mothers of disabled babies – and yet now she found herself allowing that very thing. She comforted herself that it would not be for long, however. Soon she could have him back again and they would make up for the lost time together.

She had not anticipated the reaction she got after that first stay in Edinburgh. Instead of happy smiles and a joyful welcome, little Brian would not even look at her. It tore at her heart and she left the room in tears.

I returned home with my parents with all my worst fears reinforced. There in the cot lay my new baby sister, born during the time I had been away. Perhaps she had taken my place in the family. She had ordinary arms . . .

3

Like all the others?

I discovered that being at home did not mean that I could forget the hated 'arms' forever. As I settled in once again and prepared to get back to the carefree life I used to lead, I found that my mother did not intend to let the matter of 'arms' drop. To begin with, as soon as we arrived home, all the neighbours came round to have a look at the 'arms'. Their amazement at what technology could do, and their delight at seeing me now with arms helped to reinforce my mother's resolve for me to grow up 'normal'.

It seemed that I was supposed to wear these horrible things and try to use them all the time. And not only that – it became clear as time went by that I would have to return to Edinburgh every four to six months in order to be refitted with new arms which had to be altered or changed as I grew. The technicians continued to attempt to make improvements to the design, and I had several different types of arms over the years. None improved my opinion of them.

I did everything I could think of to avoid the daily torture. I was supposed to wear them for seven or eight hours each day, but I would never put them on voluntarily. My mother always had to 'remind' me. I did not understand that she anguished over having to keep on at me about practising with the arms. She could see how they upset me by slowing me down, restricting all movement and causing me quite a lot of pain, but she had been told that only by constant use and practice would I be able to come to terms with them. She felt compelled to persuade me to use them, anyway, because they would improve my quality of life, wouldn't they? So much effort and money had been put into acquiring this opportunity for me, that she felt obliged to go along with the experiment – at least for a reasonable time.

'Put your arms on, Brian, there's a good boy,' she would coax as I went out to play. 'Show them to your little friends – they haven't got anything like that.' She tried to make them sound special, but I was not persuaded. I had been special enough without false arms – I could not see why I had to prove I was special by this strange addition. All I knew was that they would stop me playing because I would have to think hard every moment about how to move my shoulders so that the arms would do what I wanted them to do. How could I concentrate on cricket if I had to concentrate on making an arm move in the right direction? I could have hit the ball so much more easily with my foot.

Time and time again, I would run to my mother with tears of frustration and pain streaming down my face.

'Oh, come on then,' she would say, 'let's get those arms off.' And as my face lit up in relief, she would undo the straps only to find large blisters and sores on my shoulders where they had rubbed – red, raw weals which would take days to heal. It made me cross and depressed, and yet sometimes I even felt the sores were worth it because it meant I did not have to wear the arms for a while.

Mealtimes, too, now became a problem. Instead of being able to get on with my meal, holding a spoon in my toes, I had to use the 'arms'. A fork or spoon would have a ring welded on it so that it could be attached to the hook on the end of the right arm; or else it was fastened on with an elastic band. Then I had to get the shoulder pads working with just sufficient pressure to synchronise the two together so the fork or spoon would move up to my mouth. Of course, the process was painstakingly slow, and mistakes frequent. Sometimes the arm would fly up so the food flipped off and splattered all over the wall – or on to someone else, or else the fork would fall off the hook and I had to wait for someone to come and fix it back on again. If I could, I would wait until no one was looking, then pick up my fork or spoon with my toes and finish off my food as fast as possible!

The only amusement I ever got with them happened when inquisitive children wanted to see how the gripper 'hand' worked, and then I would hold on to their hands and not let go! The startled children would eventually be allowed to run, crying, home to their mum, who would later complain about Brian's bad behaviour!

Although the agility of any child having to submit to wearing this kind of prosthesis was clearly hampered, the authorities were conscious of the fact that a lot of time and money had gone into the development of artificial limbs. They were not prepared to see the effort go to waste. Every six weeks, therefore, a district nurse came around to see how I and other children with similar problems in our area were managing with their prostheses. Having avoided using mine as much as possible, my mother and I were necessarily wary when her visit became due. It was at this point that Laddie, the sheepdog, proved his undoubted worth.

Laddie was my special friend, and he allowed me to take all kinds of liberties with him. I could pull his tail or his ears, rub his tummy – rather roughly, I'm afraid, before I grew old enough to understand – and yet Laddie seemed to enjoy every minute. My mother knew that while Laddie and I were together, she had no fears for my safety, because he would be an ardent protector at all times.

He was also a very effective family guard dog. No matter who approached our front door, Laddie seemed to know at least two or three minutes before the knock came, and he would set up a loud barking which left us in no doubt that we had a visitor. He also liked chasing cars. Nowadays this might be a problem, but in the early 1960s in the countryside where we lived, cars were rather rare, and Laddie's outbursts were largely tolerated. As far as we were concerned, as soon as Laddie began to bark, we knew that someone was approaching, and these warnings proved never more welcome than when the district nurse came to check up on my progress.

As my mother gradually saw that wearing the arms caused me great anguish, she often colluded with me in avoiding their use. Most of the time they finished up in a cupboard, out of sight and out of mind, only to be brought out when a visitor called or when Mum's conscience told her that we should make a little more effort – and this usually coincided with an expected visit of the district nurse. I would protest when Mum suggested that I really ought to try again, oblivious to her anxiety that the district nurse would expect to see some signs of progress. As time went by, I usually won any battle in this direction and the arms were returned, unused, to the cupboard. But at the appropriate time, suddenly we would hear Laddie's frantic barking as he chased another car down the road, and Mum would just as frantically rush for the cupboard and retrieve the offending arms.

'Quickly!' she would say. 'Get these on before the nurse arrives!'

The puzzled look on the nurse's face when she saw that my ability to use the arms had not improved at all since her last visit always gave us a pang of guilt and Mum, at least, aimed to do better. It seemed strange to the nurse, too, that we always, dutifully, needed fresh supplies of gas cylinder because the last ones had been used up. How could it be that I had not improved – again – when enough use had been made of the arms to empty all the cylinders?

Innocently I looked on as the nurse handed over yet another case of new gas cylinders. Not so innocently my mother nervously accepted them with grateful thanks. Then when the nurse had gone, Mum tried not to join me in guilty giggles that we had got away with our deception once more. We just did not have the courage to confess that Mum had discovered a way of emptying the cylinders without my having to suffer by using the arms. In a moment of inspiration, she had taken a case of cylinders to the back yard, and with the help of the fireside poker, we had managed together to press the valve on each which released the gas. Unfortunately, the gas that escaped was not of an invisible kind, but consisted of a white foam which seemed to expand as it met the air. When Dad arrived home from work, he was completely baffled as to why the whole backyard appeared to be covered with white in the middle of summer!

For a while after the nurse's visit, Mum would have an attack of conscience and insist that I put on the arms. One trick I used to get rid of the gas and make it look as though I had been practising was to get my sister Pat to keep pressing the pressure pads for me. This would make the arms wave vigorously up and down, and it used to make us laugh at first, but before long, Pat would get fed up with keeping on pressing, and protest. I had to bribe her with sweets to get her to keep going!

I never managed to last long with the arms before frustration and anger set in. When I could stand it no longer, I tried to find an ultimate solution. Going round the house beyond my mother's hearing, I slammed the arms up against a wall. Furiously I swung the hateful arms – again and again, crash after crash, putting all my strength and hatred into each smash, willing them to disintegrate and relieve me of their constant threat. Sadly, either I did not possess enough strength, or else they were made with the rough ways of little boys in mind, because although I may have bent them a bit, I did not manage to do a great deal of damage – except to the wall!

Although my mother's attitude softened to some extent with regard to making me wear the arms, she was still burdened with trying to encourage me to make some effort. Her continual urging led to a lot of difficulties between us as she tried to cope with a sullen, irritable child in place of the happy, cheerful little boy I used to be. At one time nothing would deter me from doing anything I really wanted to do, but now she had to contend with a child who would go to any lengths to avoid having to wear 'arms', and who became listless and withdrawn when made to wear them.

'No! I won't wear them!' I would shout as Mum gently suggested another try.

'Come, on, love,' she coaxed, 'what will the nurse say if you haven't got any better by the time she comes next?'

'I don't care!' I shouted back. 'Take them away!'

'But you must try,' she attempted again, and then as I went to run from her, in frustration she would get angry. 'Now come here and put these on, and don't let's have all this fuss. You *must* try!' And as she tried to grab me, I would throw myself on the floor and kick my legs in fury. I shouted, screamed and displayed temper tantrums which left us both distressed, but fear of hospital recriminations and a fear for my future compelled her to persist.

Gradually my resistance was eroded and I blandly complied when I had to. But it took its toll in reducing my confidence. The ogre of being not acceptable in my natural state surfaced and reduced my feelings of self-worth. The arms became a symbol of something I ought to be and yet could never achieve and I descended into despair.

The inevitable trips to Edinburgh came round with monotonous regularity. My heart sank as the date neared, but all the excuses I could muster to avoid the trips were to no avail. My mother still felt obliged to make some kind of attempt at encouraging me to keep on with the treatment, so off we would go yet again.

As I grew older, I was allowed a little more independence at the clinic, and although I necessarily had to wear the arms in the company of the nurses and doctors, there were one or two activities I nevertheless enjoyed. My favourite was using the hydro-pool. Swimming activities were aimed at improving muscle control and suppleness, and whatever the usefulness – or not – of artificial arms, my legs, feet and toes would always need to be at their peak of condition.

My exercises in the pool were monitored by the physiotherapist who would give me a brown, horseshoe-shaped rubber ring to put around my neck to help keep me afloat and then, lying back in the water, with her arms giving some support under my body, she showed me how to kick with my legs and so move backwards. I loved these games, and willingly co-operated – for a change! I became more confident when I discovered how to hang on to the side of the pool with my toes. I could take a breather this way, and relax for a moment or two.

During one of these sessions when I was seven years old, my heart nearly stopped with fear as I did a quick turn and my rubber ring slipped off. Terror seized me as I began to sink. I had never been in the water before without some form of support, and all the children I had seen swimming had two natural arms and legs. As I sank to the bottom, instinctively I began to kick my legs with every fraction of strength I possessed. To my relief and amazement I suddenly found myself breaking the surface. At that moment I realised I could swim! Why did I need arms? I could swim like anybody else! I never needed a rubber ring after that, and the new success boosted my confidence enormously.

Back at home I attended the day nursery in Belfast ten miles away, five days each week. It was housed in an old Nissen hut that had been used in the war, but now it had been transformed into a play centre for children with disabilities, many of them caused by thalidomide. Various organisations had donated toys and equipment to this cause, and consequently the playroom was crammed with toys of every description – tricycles, slides, building sets and specialised equipment designed to help children with disabilities.

I would have delighted in my daily outings to the nursery if it had not been for the fact that I discovered I was expected to wear the arms while there. It was hoped that children with similar disabilities would together be encouraged to get used to their prostheses and learn to use them effectively. In the event, all we shared was anger and frustration, for hardly any of the children took to wearing their false limbs happily. Even very young children possess the faculty of making some good out of bad, and a sense of humour surfaced while we fumed in our restriction.

It was at home that I discovered a new game when I wore the arms. Instead of wasting time while my food got cold before I could eat it, I found that the gripper 'hand' could be flicked in a certain way so that a spoonful of peas could be sent flying over my head. It became great fun to see if I could beat my previous record for distance flicking! Laddie quickly learned that if he stationed himself near me when I wore the arms at the dinner table, then he could pick up a few titbits, and would look expectantly at me when the arms came out of the cupboard.

It was but a short step for me to teach the children this new fun at nursery school, and they joined in with a will. We had contests to see who could shoot peas the farthest! Between us we found all sorts of ways to abuse our food and the false limbs, giggling delightedly at each new discovery, until we exhausted our ideas or our gas cylinders ran out leaving us helpless. If we managed to eat our dinners, the staff would thoughtfully reward us with ice cream. This simply became a race to get the ice cream into our mouths before it melted and covered both the floor and us!

Every few months, the mothers would be invited to meet together and share their successes and failures. My mother enjoyed these times of sharing and picked up tips to help both her and me, not the least of which was the swopping of knitting patterns. In those early days Mum would not bother to knit sleeves into my jumpers – it didn't seem worth it – but she soon discovered that I needed special clothes at the nursery to stand up to the battering they got as I flung myself into play. She therefore bought me good, hard-wearing shirts and trousers especially for the purpose. As soon as we got home, however, off would come the good clothes and on would go cheaper, home-made ones that could be replaced easily if they wore into holes.

I resented having to take off my nice, new clothes, and one day resolved to do something about it. While my mother baked cakes in the kitchen, I began to remove my old things. I had to twist my supple legs upwards and with my feet, gradually ease my jumper up and over my head. It took me some time, but I did it. Then I turned to my trousers.

Out in the kitchen, my mother suddenly realised that I was very quiet. Peeping in at the door, she watched me in amazement. That it could be possible for me to dress or undress myself had not occurred to her at all. She waited, fascinated, to see how I would tackle the problem of removing my own trousers.

It was no easy task. I had to twist my foot up and get it into the elastic waistband of the trousers, and then wriggle about to inch them down little by little. Time and again they would slip out of my grasp and revert back to their position, but I did not give up. Hot with effort and with perspiration dripping down my face, I kept on until I managed to get the waistband over my hips. The rest was comparatively easy as I stood up and wriggled the trousers to the ground. But I was not finished yet. I had to get the new trousers which were in the drawer of the cabinet. I lifted up my foot and pulled the drawer open, then grabbed the trousers with my teeth.

My mother watched to see what I would do next. How could a child with no arms possibly manage to put on his own trousers? It took me a long while, but after wriggling about and pulling with my teeth, I finally got the trousers on. In relief and satisfaction I sat back, delighted with my achievement.

'Well done!' exclaimed my mother, clapping her hands. 'You are a clever boy!'

I beamed at her. It certainly felt good to manage a new task all by myself.

'I am sorry, though,' she went on, 'I'm afraid you can't wear those trousers to play around here. They will have to come off again.'

I looked at her in disbelief. Surely she wouldn't make me take them off after all my efforts to put them on? But Mum was adamant. The trousers would have to come off. My delight changed to fury and I kicked and screamed as she put my old

34

clothes back on again. I would not attempt that trick again.

Climbing never held any fears for me. It simply meant that I had to make sure of my balance so that I didn't fall. On one occasion I nearly came to grief through my persistent climbing. I was not quite two years old at the time and decided that I did not want to wait for my mother to come in from feeding the hens before I could have a biscuit. I would get one for myself. The fact that I had to climb on to the cabinet to get it did not deter me in the least. I pushed and pulled a chair to the cabinet, heaved myself on to it, and then climbed on to the cabinet work top. Then I had to lift up one foot to open the cabinet door. This time, however, I lost my balance and fell on to the hard floor below with a sickening thud.

Hearing the sound, my mother hurried in to see what I had done, and to her horror she saw me lying apparently lifeless on the floor. She picked me up and put me in my cot, then rushed down the road to her friend and neighbour.

'Lily! Lily!' she screamed. 'Come quickly, Brian's dead!'

'Surely not,' responded her friend.

'Yes, he is! He must have fallen badly in the kitchen, and now he's dead!'

In panic, the two of them ran back to our house. Coming through the front door they were met by the sight of the 'dead' boy jumping up and down in the cot and laughing joyfully to see them! I did not seem much the worse for my experience, except for a large black and blue bruise on the side of my head. My mother's relief knew no bounds, but she did not want to risk a similar happening, so enquiries were made, and before long I was given a padded helmet which would cushion any future falls and protect my head.

When I was old enough, I particularly liked playing across the fields and beside the burn with my brother and sisters. I could take Laddie, my beloved sheepdog, with me here because it lay well away from the road and its irresistible cars. The route was also used as a shortcut to Ballyclare market, so it was a well-worn path, but as children we often met together by the burn to play. Many were the times I slipped and fell into the water, but I never thought of running home to change – I would play on, soaking wet! My mother fretted about 'catching cold', but usually the play was more important to me than the risk of 'catching cold'.

There would always be one or two children fishing in the clear stream, but they could not hope for anything bigger than a few tiddlers – usually, that is. Only once did the word get around that something bigger was available for the taking. There had been an escape at a trout farm, further up the burn. Very quickly, local fishermen gathered to try their luck. I determined not to miss the fun, and so tagged along with Alan and our big brother Derek, but this was to be serious fishing, not the bent-pin or cheap-net variety, so I perched myself on a rock to watch what they did. The stream was swollen and fast running after heavy rain, but the excitement ran high as they found that just about as soon as the hook hit the water, a trout seemed to jump on the line! We came triumphantly home with enough trout to ensure that for the next few months, Mum's ingenuity for finding new fish recipes would be stretched to the limit!

Hide-and-seek and cowboys and Indians were our most popular choice of games when we played by the burn, but since we did not possess toy guns, we used pieces of stick which I held under my chin. We had hours of pleasure in those trouble-free days when children could safely be allowed out on their own to play. The only real hazard I ever knew was in making sure Laddie did not get into trouble. Laddie used to accompany me everywhere, but all that changed when he committed the unpardonable sin. He chased the sheep. It was all very natural to him, a sheepdog, and I'm sure he didn't mean to harm them. He simply did what comes naturally and tried to herd them. The farmer did not see it like that, though. That evening he appeared at our house with a loaded gun.

'One of my sheep has been killed,' he said, angrily. 'I know your dog has been around them, and he'll have to be shot.'

We crowded around Laddie in terror. I could not imagine a worse tragedy than to have my beloved dog killed. My parents argued for his life, pointing out that he did not kill sheep – just perhaps herd them a little. The farmer took some time to be convinced, but in the end he compromised.

'Let me see that dog near my sheep ever again, and I'll shoot him on the spot!' he pronounced, charging off angrily. From that time on, Laddie was only allowed in and around our smallholding, but I suffered agonies of fear in case he should escape and be killed.

On all occasions when my sister Pat was around, she took on the self-appointed role of looking after me. At mealtimes I usually managed the best way I could, but Pat often took on a caring role where I was concerned and tried to help me. One of my weaknesses was bread spread with maple syrup. As I grew, I learned to spread my own bread, but sometimes Pat would do it for me. I allowed this, except when she insisted on licking the knife while she spread the maple syrup. I considered this revolting, and when I had acquired enough language, I complained in no uncertain terms. 'I'm not having that piece of bread with Pat's germs all over the knife!' I yelled, and Mum would have to come and settle the squabble.

Usually I could look after myself in a quarrel. My arms may have been missing, but where other children used their fists in defence, I used my shoulders which were hard knobs of bone where my arms ought to have been. Any child causing trouble to my brother and sisters or to me would soon discover that my 'boneyos' were not to be trifled with. Under extreme provocation I would launch into the offender with an aimed 'boneyo', causing dire damage. In later years I thought back on those 'boneyo' attacks with some embarrassment, but they certainly left no doubt that I was willing and able to defend myself.

I don't know what mischief I would have got myself into if Pat had not been so careful for me, but I did not always appreciate her help. And sometimes I drove her to distraction. Her favourite toy was a green dolls' pram with a suede-covered hood. She loved to arrange her dolls comfortably inside and take them for a walk down the lane. I would watch her holding the handle with her hands, and wonder how I could get to do something like that. I did not wonder for long. I soon found that if I shoved my head under the handle and pushed with my chest then I, too, could move the pram round the yard. However, the comfort of the dolls did not rate highly on my priority list. My interest lay in racing it like a car. I shot off, with no idea about steering or direction.

Thump! The pram crashed into the pigsty. I manoeuvred it into a better position for a straight run and off we went again. Smash! With my head down, I could not negotiate corners, and into the side of the house we went, chipping the shiny green paint from the front of the pram.

'Mummy!' yelled Pat. 'Brian's banging my pram into everything! He's spoiling it!'

Mum would rush out and warn me not to touch the beloved pram, and for a time I would be thwarted. Not for long, though. My memory seemed short in this respect, and I would soon be transgressing again. The poor pram had a short life, but it lived on through its wheels that became part of a go-kart. My half-brother Derek and my brother Alan made a superb specimen that sported an effective foot brake.

On the day of its completion, my sister, brother and I, together with the five children of a neighbour, all trooped off to a nearby hill where, to my frustration, everyone else had a go before me. The kart had a rope attached to the front wheel axle to provide steering. The others held the rope with their hands and worked the brake with their feet, but I had to find another method. When, at last, my turn came, I had worked it out. With my feet firmly on either side of the front axle, I could steer well. Alan gave me a push to start me off, and down the hill I flew.

It was wonderful! Halfway down the hill, with the end careering towards me, I realised that I had not thought about the brake. I had no spare feet to work it.

'Steer into the ditch!' shouted someone as they saw my dilemma. Into the ditch I went, fearing for the safety – not of myself, but of the precious go-kart. I dreaded to think what the others would say if I wrecked it at my first go. As they pulled me out, I heard no cries of anger, and breathed a sigh of relief when all seemed well.

They would not risk the same thing happening again, though. When my turn came round again, someone sat behind me to steer, while I activated the brake. I enjoyed this probably as much as if I drove it alone. We screamed in delight as we tore down the hill.

It was a wonder that my feet were not covered in scars. My ten toes were more important to me than anyone could possibly imagine, and yet I hated wearing socks and shoes. I wanted to be ready with my toes for every eventuality, just as others have their hands free.

By the age of two or three I could already use my toes almost as well as my brother and sister could use their fingers, but my feet had a double purpose. I had to walk on my 'fingers'. Now and again, my mother had to insist that I wore shoes and socks, but I hated it. Off they would come as soon as possible. I felt confined with my feet encased, so come rain or shine, stones or gravel, I would throw off the hated shoes and socks and leave my toes free to explore.

On Sundays, however, we did not go off together to play. Although my parents were not particularly religious, Sunday had an atmosphere all its own. In Northern Ireland even nowadays a strong tradition of church attendance persists, but in the 1960s, it was even stronger. Most people went to church twice on a Sunday, but many went up to four times in the one day. Perhaps the care of the animals on our smallholding made attending church difficult for my parents, but they insisted that all their children went to Sunday school – besides, it gave them peace and quiet for an hour or so!

In the morning, the children were accommodated separately and my teacher happened to be Pastor Young's daughter. It took very little to please children in those pre-computer days, and I just couldn't wait to get there to show how well I could draw and colour the Bible-story pictures with my toes.

But that was not the end of our religious training. After the obligatory Sunday roast lunch, a friend from another church just a mile down the road would collect us all and take us off to his church where Sunday school took place in the afternoon. This was a Brethren gathering, and therefore rather more lively than the Presbyterian service we went to in the mornings. We just loved the happy songs we learned – often complete with actions and a lot of fun. We were obliged to learn a memory verse, but we didn't mind that because we got sweets as a reward! The greatest reward for our efforts, however, came one Sunday in the year when we were presented with prizes according to the marks we had gained. This was Prize Giving Sunday when marks for attendance and learning the memory verses would be counted up. We then received a book valued according to the number of marks we had acquired. I loved these books and looked forward to them eagerly. When I got older I was given a Bible with a zip-fastener all round it. This was a prize, indeed, and one I cherished for many years.

On one Sunday morning, however, we were unable to go to Sunday school. Mum had got me ready first, and then turned her attention to my baby sister Gwen. She had to be bathed in the tin tub beside the fire in the living-room. Perhaps I was a bit excited about the forthcoming outing to church, but inadvertently I tripped on the rug and fell heavily against the fireside hearth. Horrified, my mother saw that I had cut my ear badly. Quickly placing Gwen down safely, she grabbed a towel as my ear began to stream blood. Wrapping me up in it, the towel was soon soaked and it became clear that it would need the attention of a doctor. Leaving Dad with the rest of the children, Mum bundled me into my big brother Derek's car and he rushed us round to the surgery. As soon as the doctor saw the extent of the cut he advised a ten-mile drive to the children's hospital in Belfast. The cut required eight stitches, and it affected my hearing from that time on.

Pastor Young used to keep in contact with my parents by calling round to the house every so often. He tried to encourage my mother by marvelling at my progress, but his amazement was genuine as he saw the little toddler climb up on to the settee without the use of arms. Then, when I later had the mechanical arms he could not hide his admiration as I performed one of my exercises for him by picking up little wooden buttons with the hook on the end of my arm, and placing them into a jar. By the time I had finished, beads of perspiration were standing on my brow, and I was hot with the effort.

'He's marvellous!' he would say. 'Such determination! What a great little chap!'

My mother loved to hear the praise, but deep within she still wondered whether I would ever be able to cope in an adult world.

4

Going to school

As I approached school age, enquiries were made as to which school would suit me best. My brother Alan and sister Pat both went to Ballylinney Primary School not far from our home, and it was decided that I should spend a trial period there. A typical little country school of the time, it possessed just one classroom, an asphalt playground, outside toilets and a teaching staff of one – Miss Montgomery, who had sole responsibility for all the twenty-six pupils.

I would walk to school wearing my padded helmet, just in case I got into mischief with Alan and Pat on the way, but once there I had no fears about managing like all the others – so long as I didn't have to wear the 'arms'. Not many concessions were made to what others saw as my disability – and that was how I liked it. I had a desk like everyone else, but I also had a square of carpet so that I could sit comfortably on the wooden floorboards whenever necessary.

The children watched, fascinated at first, as Miss Montgomery showed me how to write and draw with a pencil between my toes and also with the paintbrush to paint pictures. Soon the novelty wore off, however, and we all got on with our lessons. When breaktime came round I held my little bottle of milk in my feet to drink with the straw, and then in the playground the children were very protective of me as I joined in all their games.

I loved all my lessons, but drawing, painting and doing sums were special favourites; then at lunchtime we all sat together in the classroom to eat our sandwiches. Sometimes I had an orange, too, peeling it deftly with my toes and enjoying Miss Montgomery's look of wonder and admiration as I did it.

It came, therefore, as a disappointment to me to be told after six months that I would have to leave the school and go somewhere else. Apparently it was thought that I ought to have better facilities than the little school could provide.

Miss Montgomery and my parents, therefore, had visited the Fleming Fulton School for children with physical disabilities in Belfast in order to see if this would be a better choice for me. They had been invited, originally, to hear the inspiring talk of a Mr Wilkie, from the United States, who also had been born without arms and who had overcome his disability to live a full and useful life. As he told his story, they watched, amazed, as with his toes, he took a wallet from his pocket and counted out the notes! My parents had not considered such dexterity possible. They assumed that artificial arms were the gateway to full mobility if only I could be persuaded to persevere with them.

The Fleming Fulton School had been named after a doctor who had been the first medical officer for schools in Belfast, and also the chairman of the Orthopaedic Council. It was the first time any education authority had set up a school with interdisciplinary staff consisting of a team of teachers together with physiotherapists, occupational and speech therapists, medical officers, nurses, child-care and residential staff. It opened in 1957 with twenty-three pupils, but by the time I arrived, there were 137, including nine thalidomides. The total was to rise in the 1970s to around 220. Three children were admitted from the City Hospital Nursery Unit in 1966: David Loughran, George Cherry and myself. We were to become lifelong friends.

The authorities provided our transport, a taxi delivering us in the mornings, and returning us home each afternoon. At first five of us were crammed into the car – together with George's wheelchair – for the ten-mile journey to school. However, one morning it transpired that the car door had not been securely locked, for as we drove into the school driveway, the door flew open and George was thrown out almost into the path of the deputy headteacher's car following! When George's mother found out what had happened, she complained bitterly to the taxi company, and soon after we were provided with a minibus complete with proper wheelchair lift.

On another occasion, the taxi company overbooked and left us without transport to take us home. After an hour's delay, the only alternative they could come up with was a huge black hearse! Our parents were all beside themselves with worry when after an hour we had still not returned home. Their anxieties still were not relieved by seeing a hearse pull up at the door!

Often, particularly in snowy weather, the minibus arrived for us long before the set time. It may have been that they had other bookings to fit in, but on bad days we were sometimes collected well before seven o'clock in the morning – and occasionally even before we got out of bed! Mum had to rush round getting me a piece of toast to eat on the way, and then we would arrive at school at least an hour before everyone else! If the snow fell deeply, however, the road would be blocked and our way to school impossible. We loved these times because it meant we could all meet together with our toboggans and have a few days of glorious fun until the snow thawed enough for the minibus to get through.

The Fleming Fulton School was custom-built for the needs of children without limbs. There were no desks, but instead we each had a table high enough to take a wheelchair or to reach up to with a foot. The subjects offered matched those of an ordinary school, but we necessarily worked at a slower pace because most children needed help with writing. A care assistant – at a rate of one to each twelve children – was on hand to assist, but therapists helped with the all-important 'life skills' lessons when we practised exercises in mobility suitable to our disabilities.

I never found a great deal of trouble learning, providing I could be allowed to get on with writing in my own way, but here at Fleming Fulton wearing the arms was compulsory. This led to the utmost frustration, as I had to slow down to the length of time it took me to co-ordinate the arms so that I could actually get something down on paper.

As time went by, I gave in to the struggle with the arms. I could not do all the schoolwork necessary and use the arms at the same time, and since all the adults around me seemed to think that the arms were more important, my schoolwork had to suffer. I found this very difficult to come to terms with because I knew I could do more or less anything if only I could be allowed to use my toes. I consequently became dejected, sulky and petulant.

Mrs Thompson, the senior physiotherapist, had been sent to Heidelberg University Hospital, in Germany, to study their methods of helping limbless children. She knew that in the British Isles the thalidomide catastrophe had affected several hundred children, but she discovered with astonishment that in Germany the total had reached several thousand! The extent of the problem led to a great deal of research into the best ways to help these tragic children.

Mrs Thompson learned a lot in Heidelberg and returned with her concept of physiotherapy completely transformed. She could not supply us with all the specialist equipment she had seen there, but she did introduce us to a large plastic ball that we would roll or push in various ways to help develop muscles and improve overall balance.

She saw my particular need to be in the development of stomach and shoulder muscles with the aim of a better use of artificial arms. Most people use their shoulders only in relation to their arms, but my shoulders had to be used independently with upward, backward and forward movements so that I could effectively activate the pressure pads. One way to achieve this aim came through using another heavy kind of ball which I had to roll up my legs on to my stomach – not once, but ten times in a row! After this followed thirty sit-ups – press-ups without arms. It meant lifting my head and torso with Mrs Thompson pressing downwards to make it more difficult. The session often finished with jogging on the spot for ten minutes while Mrs Thompson called out, 'Keep those legs up high, Brian!' I would perspire profusely, my head compensating for the lack of sweat glands under the arms.

However, her concern did not only lie in encouraging me to use the arms. She also wanted me to develop a wider range of movements; the better to be able to perform all those tasks which others do with their hands. I dreaded these exercises more than the others. I had to lie on my back and stretch for small blocks which I had to lift with my toes, then swing them over and across to drop them into a container which was always a little higher and further away than before. Mrs Thompson would urge me on, saying, 'A little bit more, just a little bit more . . .' and I would wince in agony. I realise now how important these exercises were, but I did not appreciate them then!

As a truly dedicated teacher, Mrs Thompson went to a great deal of trouble to do the best for her children. She heard that horse-riding achieved good results with handicapped children by giving them more confidence, balance and posture. So, before raising the matter with the authorities, she took riding lessons herself first for a year, and then suggested that we should all have the opportunity.

It proved to be a wonderful experience. We loved our riding lessons, although most of us were quite nervous at first, being either unable to hold on with hands or grip with legs. In my case, the reins were adapted by being cut in half and having one put on each of the stirrups, so that I could direct the horse to the left or right by kicking the appropriate leg. My only problem seemed to be getting a lively horse to slow down!

There were still lessons to be learned about safety, however. Poor Mrs Thompson suffered agonies when the hook on the artificial arms of my friend David Loughran got caught up in the stirrups and he was dragged, hanging from his horse for some distance. From that day on, all artificial limbs had to be removed before riding lessons. That made the lessons even more attractive to me.

'Life skills' lessons covered a multitude of tasks. One of them was the basic need for us to be able to dress ourselves. We could never be fully independent without this obvious skill. Miss Martin, our therapist for this subject, had tried for years to puzzle out a way by which children with no arms could do up their own zips, buttons, hooks and eyes. She introduced us to all sorts of devices: rings, straps, elastic bands, strings and loops inside the trouser leg, plus wire coat hangers for all manner of uses. Weird and wonderful ideas which certainly helped, but none so much as the 'magic' invention which broke on to the market in the 1960s: Velcro. When this wonder tape came into being, suddenly Miss Martin's little charges had a chance of independence. We still had to struggle and wriggle to get our trousers on, but once there, doing them up became much easier. I wonder if the inventor knew how grateful we all were to him – and still are!

In later years, with the experience of maturity, I discovered that if I bought my trousers one size too large, then they would be much easier to pull up, and I learned to pull up the zip with my toes, so I opt for this most of the time now. Putting on a shirt has always been a tricky job, however. As children we used to try all sorts of ways. Once on, Velcro fastenings were easy, but the Velcro showed on the front so it was not popular as we got older. If we wore clothes with zips, sometimes the zip tag had a large hoop attached so we could pull it up with our toes. Unfortunately our toes occasionally got stuck in the hoop and we had to be contortionists to free ourselves!

I thought I had found a good method of putting on a shirt. I would button it up with my toes first, then throw it up into the air so that as it ballooned down, I could manoeuvre my head into it. It was as tricky as it sounds and I'm afraid failures outnumbered successes and I got tired of trying! Nowadays I lay out my shirt with all except the top two buttons fastened, then opening the bottom with my teeth, I tuck my head into it and wriggle about until the shirt falls over my head. It does so about 95 per cent of the time. Occasionally, of course, it falls on back to front, but I am adept at twisting my body so that the shirt comes round the right way. To begin with I used to get myself all mixed up by managing to get my head in the armholes!

The one thing I cannot do is to tuck my shirt into my trousers. I hate to have to admit it, but this small thing has beaten me and there have been times when I have missed an appointment rather than turn up with my shirt hanging out! If I need to look particularly smart I sometimes wear a jumper that covers the end of my shirt, but there is no way I can tuck it in for myself!

Shoes and socks have always presented a problem to me – not because I can't put them on, but because I don't want them on! At Fleming Fulton we were always required to wear shoes and socks, but the shoes had to be slip-on ones so they could be removed whenever necessary. It did not happen as often as I would have liked because I was forced to practise with the arms most of the time. To me, my toes are my 'fingers'. I use them – and want to use them – like most people use their natural fingers. Therefore, I need to have my feet free and available at all times – in the same way that hands are free. Imagine what it would be like if those with hands had to wear gloves, only to remove them every time they wanted to eat something, pick up a piece of paper or book, or do the million and one tasks that have to be done daily. It would be very tiresome indeed and they would, no doubt, constantly ask 'Why?' Similarly, I asked, 'Why?' Why did I have to keep taking off and putting on my socks and shoes when it would be so much easier to keep them free? Why did I have to wear arms when my legs and toes were more efficient? After I left school I put away socks forever, and shoes for all except essential times. Since I do not like the look of slip-on shoes, I make sure now that my shoelaces are always done up but just loose enough to allow me to slip the shoes on and off easily.

I learned other everyday tasks without much trouble. When I got up in the mornings, before I had to put my arms on I could wash by holding the flannel in my toes, reaching my face with increasing ease, as my hips became more and more supple. Holding a bar of soap was a bit tricky, although I got to grips with it, so to speak, before long! I also learned to comb my hair – I can easily reach my head with my toes – and I cleaned my own teeth. In my early years I was given a battery-powered toothbrush, but I can hold an ordinary toothbrush perfectly well in my toes.

Toilet training proved rather difficult when I was too young to deal with my trousers, and I necessarily had to have someone to help me dress. I determined to overcome that obstacle, however, and made a concerted effort to manage my own trousers.

It did not take me very long to become proficient, and the independence that followed was very satisfying. Needless to say, if I had followed instructions and used my artificial arms, I would probably still be trying to gain my independence!

I looked forward to the holidays eagerly. Although my mother still thought that false arms were the key to my becoming fully independent and able to – hopefully – find a job, I could usually avoid wearing them for most of the time. Holidays therefore gave me a longed-for respite in the continual frustration.

Until 1967, all our family holidays had been taken in a caravan at Portrush, but in this memorable year everything changed. We were going in an aeroplane to the Isle of Man! My previous experience of flying had not been good – the air pressure always affected my sensitive ears – but this would not be a long flight, and anyway, we were going on holiday, not to take me for tortuous training at the hospital unit. We all looked forward to our wonderful time away, and counted the days until it would arrive.

The Isle of Man may only have been a short way away across the Irish Sea, but to us it seemed like going 'abroad'. We arrived, carrying all our luggage, at our destination of Douglas, and proceeded to search out the Bayview guest-house, where we would be staying for the next two weeks. We found it in a prime position on the seafront, and excitedly settled in.

I had hoped that since we were supposed to be on holiday, I would be granted a holiday from wearing arms, but Mum would have none of it. We were going to be meeting lots of new people – other guests in the guest-house, strangers on the beach – we didn't want to embarrass them by seeing a child with no arms, did we? It would be much kinder to them to wear the arms – and to me, of course, in the end, thought Mum.

I considered the arms were so horrible that they would be just as much a shock to a stranger as a child with no arms at all. I couldn't see the point in the argument, but I knew I would have to wear them, so I made the best of it.

When we all trooped into the dining-room for breakfast the next morning, my arms were strapped on firmly. I could manage quite a lot with them by now – albeit slowly – so I could be confident of actually getting something to eat, but they continued to be very uncomfortable, and I still had to concentrate hard to make them work properly. The constant fear was that the gas cylinder would run out and leave me looking foolish with outstretched arms. I could not do much to avoid that eventuality, so I tried not to let it worry me.

I soon attracted the attention of the other guests, and they smiled admiringly as they saw me tackling my cornflakes with my mechanical arms. Never one to miss an opportunity of showing off, I played to the gallery! Mum glowed with pride, and for once in my life wearing arms did not seem quite so bad. Thereafter, I was the centre of attraction, and got to know some of the other guests very well. They even took the hazardous step of offering to look after the children while Mum and Dad went off for an evening, but I imagine our 'sitters' were very glad to see Mum and Dad return after we had practically demolished the flower-beds by playing football! Somehow, though, I always managed to get away with it!

It was not the same when we got down to the beach. The sun shone beautifully and we prepared for a long, lazy stay on the sand. My brother and sisters and I stripped off our clothes and, donning our swimsuits, ran for the sea. It was wonderful! I loved the feel of the sand and the water, and the freedom to run and play together. My mother, however, was apprehensive. As soon as I took off my shirt, she became conscious of the inquisitive, pitying glances of the people nearby, and the quiet, whispering stares as they looked at my limbless body. She could not stand it for long. Suddenly she jumped up and ran back across the road to our guest-house where she quickly found my T-shirt. For the rest of the holiday I would have to be covered up when I played on the beach.

Wherever we went – to the shops or the fun fair, the beach or a café, I seemed to attract attention. Thalidomide had only recently been in the news then, so everyone was interested to see a real-life example of what they had seen on television. I found it all quite amusing, but it could not have been so easy for the rest of the family, particularly my mother who still felt a subconscious guilt about her part in the tragedy.

I did not know it at the time, but our Isle of Man holiday was to have far-reaching implications. My parents had been very impressed with the natural beauty of the Island and although we were not able to return for another holiday, for the next three years they must have been remembering and discussing it between them. The 'Troubles' in Northern Ireland were becoming increasingly difficult to bear. Bomb scares happened frequently, and although we did not expect to be greatly affected on our smallholding in the country, one did not really know who would suffer next.

In May 1970 it came as an immense surprise to us when our parents announced the earth-shattering news that we were going to move to the Isle of Man to live. At first we were excited, but soon we realised that there would be a few snags to our new life. First, my beloved companion, Laddie, would not be able to go with us. I had not seen the blow coming, but gradually my parents made me see that Laddie was now old and ill and that it would not be a kindness to uproot him to an entirely new place. Before we left, therefore, Laddie had to be put to sleep.

I cannot express my grief at the loss of the pet who had been so close to me all my life. I was quite heartbroken, and it took me a long time to come to terms with the grief. I would never forget him, but the bustle of the move went some way to lightening my anguish.

There were other problems to overcome. We had to say goodbye to many friends, relatives and neighbours whose company we had enjoyed long before the days when television put a stop to frequent visiting and sharing. These were the people with whom we had laughed and cried and shared good times and bad. It would be a major wrench to leave them all.

Our parents, however, saw a new life with – hopefully – the opportunity of a better living in beautiful surroundings, and the prospect looked good. They had seen possibilities in the hotel trade and had bought a guest-house in a promising position. It was to be perhaps more difficult than they had anticipated, for they moved to a different guest-house at least seven times in the next ten years on the Island – including a brief time with a guest-house in Blackpool, England!

5

Back to Ireland

The first task on arrival on the Isle of Man was to install all the children into schools. Alan, Pat and Gwen were accepted immediately, but I proved more difficult. We applied to various schools, but no one felt able to provide the appropriate care for a boy with no arms. They could see that artificial arms would slow down my ability to write or, in fact, do anything, and they did not have sufficient resources to provide me with the extra help I would need. I tried to explain that if only I could be allowed to give up the arms, then I could cope with almost anything, but the adults around me still felt that artificial arms were the key to my future livelihood and insisted that I persist.

My mother had hoped that after all the time I had been using the arms, I might have got used to them by now, but still I hated them with every fibre of my being and longed to dispose of them and get on with my life. But the schools were adamant. They could not cope with a disabled child. My mother's worst fears seemed to be realised. Her Brian was always going to have trouble being accepted in the world.

Finally, they were forced to consider the Fleming Fulton School back in Belfast where I had already spent my childhood years. As an eight-year-old I took this option very badly. We were now a long way from Northern Ireland and if I had to be sent there, then I would necessarily be a boarder. How could my parents be so cruel as to send me away now? We had only just arrived in the Isle of Man and everything was so exciting. How could they even think of making me go so far away? When would I see them again?

My parents tried to explain that it would be the best place for me – that no other school could provide me with such good facilities, and that I could come home for the holidays – whenever possible, of course.

To me it was a prison sentence. They were sending me away to get me out of their sight. They were ashamed of me. They didn't love me at all. If they did, they would not insist that I keep trying to use these detestable arms – it all went to prove that I was not good enough without them.

Inevitably Fleming Fulton won, and I left my home – virtually for ever, in my childish mind – to go to boarding-school a long way away. I left my brother and sisters sadly, wishing again that I could throw away the heavy burden of arms and be allowed to go to the local school. I was sure I could cope there if I had only been given the chance.

During my first few weeks at school I suffered agonies of homesickness. I missed my family and showed it in an attitude of bad temper, lack of co-operation and real anguish. I longed to see my mother and have her assure me that arms or no arms, she really did love me and want me home again. I wanted to know that arms did not matter – that she loved Brian even if he had no arms.

It took quite a long time, but eventually I did settle to a

routine at school and made the best of it. At least it was good to meet my friends George Cherry and David Loughran again.

A maximum of twenty-four boarders were accommodated in a separate unit called 'the Chalet', set out on ground-floor level for wheelchair access and ease of movement. We had our own dining-room with octagonal tables at which the obligatory 'school' cuisine was served to us. We could always expect fishless fish cakes on Wednesday; fish and chips on Fridays; fatty Irish stew on Saturdays – of which we were forced to eat every last morsel as though in punishment; but on Sundays we could expect a roast dinner, with a pudding of jelly with hot custard. The result was always pink runny custard, but since I had to maintain a strict diet, I rarely experienced this particular joy.

That I should maintain a steady weight seemed to be very important. There had to be no restrictions to the movement of my legs and hips, and my body needed to remain sleek and supple in order to use the arms effectively. I therefore found myself denied foods which I particularly loved – sweets, puddings and cakes – and had to be content with a second best choice of fruit when most of the others were tucking into sticky puddings. For instance, my breakfast would consist of prunes, rhubarb or stewed apple instead of cereal, then half a slice of toast, but without any marmalade or jam. Sugar simply was not allowed. I had, therefore, to learn to like tea without sugar, and to endure even the rhubarb or stewed apple unsweetened. The rule no doubt applied to others who had a disability similar to mine, but it all went to reinforce my feelings of rejection and deprivation.

Pocket money was doled out rigidly once each week. A safe box in the office held money provided by our parents, but it had to cover everything – school trips, postage stamps, stationery and pens. Consequently, our allowance was necessarily small, but with it I could sometimes buy a forbidden bar of chocolate which I savoured, making it last as long as possible.

When the long-awaited holidays finally came, my mother was always so shocked at my emaciated appearance that she would fill me up with all sorts of good food designed to build me up again.

'I've got your favourite maple syrup in,' she would say. 'You can have it on toast for breakfast *and* tea if you like. Then there'll be fried potatoes whenever you want them!'

It invariably meant that by the end of the holiday, the arms harness became a tight fit, but that did not bother me. I preferred to have enough to eat and then put up with the discomfort until I got thin again. My mother used also to be horrified by the state of my hair. She would demand that Dad take me to the barber's as soon as possible to get my hair back into some order.

In spite of my opinion of the enforced diet, the school kept a close eye on our health. As in all schools, a nurse and dentist were often in attendance, and my teeth caused particular concern. I had apparently been born with too many teeth, and since they were vital to me as a means of lifting and carrying, they needed to be in peak condition. Therefore, over one particular nine-month period I had to see the dentist almost every other week for extractions and other work. I hated it, but only in later years could I understand the importance of a good set of teeth.

Another questionable touch of care came in the form of 'goodnight kisses' . . . Bedtimes were strictly applied according to age, and went up in fifteen-minute intervals. The duty member of staff would come round to each of us to tuck us in, but in deference to the fact that we were far away from home and our mothers, they would also add a goodnight kiss. I realise now that it showed a very thoughtful attitude, but we only appreciated it according to who happened to be giving it! When Miss Watson was on duty, then I would often need to be tucked in more than once, but other members of staff were not so eagerly awaited!

We each had a bedside lamp, and had to put it out when told. However, I liked to read or sometimes we wanted to talk, so we soon found that a hat, a pillow case or some such cover would dim the light enough to fool the staff into thinking we were asleep. We became adept at telling each other stories, but my friend Alan, who had a strong Christian faith, told the best stories. No matter what they were about, at some point he always managed to bring Jesus into it! His stories made me feel uncomfortable, but I listened carefully. Alan's was the kind of faith that seemed to really mean something, and yet the more I heard about Jesus, the more I wanted to know about him. Alan answered my questions gladly.

Miss Martin continued our independence training, and it was not until years later that I discovered she had not been totally convinced of the advantages to us of prosthetic limbs. She had seen just how easily the limbless children managed with whatever limbs they possessed, and she noticed the strain and stress the artificial limbs inflicted. But, she thought, everyone knew that these children must benefit from the addition of missing limbs – *mustn't they*? Surely they should persist so that they could be as 'normal' as possible in the adult world – *shouldn't they*? Gently she and the other staff persuaded us to keep on trying, but at the same time they taught us ways of doing things with our existing limbs, too.

First, we experimented with my desktop to find which angle would suit me best. We discovered that a tilt of forty-five degrees would allow me to work with my toes effectively. It also had a non-slip surface, which meant my books and pencils would not fall to the floor. Only when detailed work like that of making maps or graphs was needed did it become necessary for me to sit on the floor.

I had already learned three ways of writing: first, with a pencil trapped in the hook of my artificial arms. This necessitated having the pencil fastened on with an elastic band because with every expansion of my chest as I breathed, the hook would open and the pencil fall out. Each mark I made meant having to co-ordinate muscles all over my body in order to make the pencil move in the right direction. It might be compared to a right-handed person trying to write legibly with their left hand – except that I used shoulder and chest muscles to make the movements. I had to concentrate more on the action of writing than on what I wanted to write about!

Whenever I could, I used other methods of writing: by holding a pencil or pen between my toes and, third, with a pen between my teeth. I could not use a pencil for this method because of the danger of lead poisoning, but I became quite proficient with the pencil between my toes – although speed was a problem.

At the age of seven or eight I could only write five to ten words a minute, and after gripping the pencil for about half an hour, I would get painful cramps on the arch of my foot. Thankfully, this reduced as I grew older, and nowadays I can write just as efficiently with either my toes or my teeth – in fact, the resulting writing looks exactly the same. Throughout the years my writing has become indistinguishable from that of someone using hands and fingers.

In 1971, however, after a visit from Lady Hoare we were introduced to another method of writing. Lady Hoare had been very involved with the thalidomide tragedy from the start, and had been so touched by it that she set up the Lady Hoare Trust for Thalidomide Children, and had been working on its behalf ever since. I had already met her once during my first stay at Edinburgh when she came to look at the clinic, but now she visited us with a suggestion of practical help. A new invention had been developed which adapted typewriters for use with the toes instead of fingers. It was called a 'Possum' typewriter, and Lady Hoare had come to discuss the feasibility of its use to those of us with varying disabilities.

Developed by IBM, the Possum consisted of a typewriter with a computer box that was designed to be fixed beneath a desk or tabletop. Attached to this was a footplate with a large knob and the numbers one to eight inscribed at compass points around it. Each letter was represented by a two-number combination, and we pushed the knob between our toes from number to number. Therefore, to write my name I moved the knob to the 7 and the 5 for 'B'; to 4 and 3 for 'R'; 4 and 5 for 'I', 7 and 1 for 'A' and 2 and 1 for 'N'. In all, fifty or so number codes had to be learned before we could write anything, but it was hoped that it would eventually improve our speed.

Lastly, a lamp was very thoughtfully fixed to each unit so that we could more easily see what we were doing since we necessarily had to sit a longer distance than normal from the typewriter. In those days of early computers, the Possum was a very heavy unit, so for ease of use it came fixed to a trolley that could be moved from room to room.

To begin with it added to my frustration. The arrival of the Possums meant we had to begin all over again by learning the letter codes. However, writing with a Possum released me from having to struggle with the terrible arms, so I determined to learn fast. Eventually I reached speeds of twenty-five to thirty words per minute, and my friend George even managed forty!

As the 'Possum Project' was so new, many visitors came to see how we were getting on with it. Frequent visitors came from Ireland, but we also met people from the United States, Germany and even Japan. They seemed fascinated by our success especially, as I discovered later, since the rejection rate for artificial limbs was so high. We all loved showing off our skills to the various visitors. But we did have to get used to the terrible clattering noise of the five Possum machines as we took notes or wrote our essays. In addition, the heat generated by the machines was absolutely unbelievable and necessitated both electric fan coolers and face cloths to wipe away the perspiration from our faces. When we tried opening the fire escape door to let in fresh air on the hot summer days our typing paper would be blown all over the place, leaving our teacher in a pickle and us in fits of laughter.

I loved geography lessons. Our teacher, Miss Wells, encouraged us to try all sorts of projects, which did not include a great deal of reading. I had missed out on my reading because of all the time wasted having to learn how to manipulate the arms, so when it came to making maps and studying pictures of other countries, I excelled. Sometimes we made large relief maps in papier-mâché, which I would painstakingly build up piece by piece on the floor using my toes. Then I would paint it and add the rivers and mountains. I always got a great deal of satisfaction out of making my map as accurate as possible.

History lessons were much more difficult because they necess-arily included a lot of reading. I was humiliated and frustrated whenever I had to read aloud, and dreaded these times. However, my teachers saw my distress and decided to do something about it. Soon I found myself excused French lessons and spent the time with Miss Harrison, the deputy headteacher, who gave me extra English lessons instead. After a while I began to really get to grips with reading and consequently my history and other lessons improved.

I did not need help with playing football! I loved the game and played it at every opportunity. We would play at breaktimes, lunch-times and any other time long enough to kick a ball around and score a few goals. Two male teachers, Mr Black and Mr Story, often joined us and we would tear around furiously letting off all our pent-up steam!

Our team became very good with David Loughran and myself as something of star players. We were the ones who most often scored the goals! So Mr Story arranged some matches with local schools. I can imagine that the teams from these 'normal' schools thought they were on to a good thing by playing the 'handicapped' team – but they did not have it all easily by any means! Those of us with feet had developed their function to a high degree. Where football was concerned, we felt ourselves to be particularly competent!

We had no doubts, therefore, about the outcome of a forthcoming match with the blind school. In fact, our natural feelings of fair play surfaced to question what Mr Story had been thinking about in fixing this match. How on earth could blind boys play football at all if they couldn't see the ball? They may have feet and legs, but surely they could not be so highly tuned as ours could. It really was not fair to subject them to the humiliation of certain defeat.

The match went ahead, however, despite our misgivings, the only concession to the other team being to use a luminous orange ball with a bell in it. We began tentatively, unsure how to handle the situation, but we soon realised that these blind boys were not to be trifled with. Their accuracy in locating the ball and its direction was incredible. They needed no indulgence on our part. Before we knew it we were fighting for our credibility, and at the end of the match, we were thoroughly thrashed by their six–three win! It made us a little more sympathetic to the teams from 'normal' schools who may well have been thinking of us with the same apprehension at the start of any match.

In May 1971, however, we were to have the biggest morale booster possible. The whole Northern Ireland football team came to visit us – including, of course, my hero, George Best! Having tried to emulate him for years, no one can imagine my ecstasy in seeing and even playing football with the greatest footballer of all time! It was a wonderful day, and one that we would all remember and talk about for years to come. It took us some time to 'come down' from the heights of joy we had experienced after the visit, but lessons had to be resumed, and eventually we got back into our routine.

For one year from September 1972 we had a change of accommodation which meant quite a lot to us. Those who could manage stairs were transferred from The Chalet to Gardiner House, a property about three miles from the main school building. The Chalet was needed for the younger children and those who required wheelchair access, and we gladly looked forward to the change of scenery. It was wonderful to finish school and be taken 'home' on the minibus. It really felt like being 'out of school'.

Gardiner House was situated in a leafy, residential and relatively quiet area so different from school grounds, and we loved being there. However, a Member of Parliament lived opposite and so had a continual police presence due to the 'Troubles'. On the whole we were not affected much by Northern Ireland's long-standing problems. We had become used to it to some extent, although the windows of the Chalet were always taped in case of bomb blasts, and we were evacuated once because of a bomb scare. Some of the other children could tell a different story – bombings happened in the streets where they lived and they had seen dreadful sights.

Being one of the very few mixed schools in Ulster – that is Protestant and Catholic, not boys and girls – several of my best friends lived in either Loyalist or Nationalist strongholds, and occasionally they had to be taken home early during times of high tension. But thankfully, this happened rarely, and we enjoyed peace most of the time.

During my time at Gardiner House, I was asked if I would like to join the Boys' Brigade. The 9th Belfast Boys' Brigade Company met every Tuesday evening, and I accepted the invitation eagerly. For the next two years I looked forward to joining in all the activities possible – especially as this was a 'no false arms zone'! I would set out smartly in full uniform of dark blue jacket with brown belt and brass buckle, hat and shining black shoes, plus a white haversack, ready for the company inspection. Then we would be put through our drilling paces. I was glad that no allowances were made for the fact that I had no arms. If my kit did not look up to standard, then I would be reprimanded just like the others. The only exception to the rule was to exempt me from having to salute the senior officers. I wished that I could, like the others, but it was a small price to pay for the satisfaction of not having to wear the arms.

I have to admit, however, that in one instance I did think that wearing the arms might – but only *might* – be a good idea. During the second part of the evening the hall would be transformed into a gymnasium with climbing frames, ropes, rings, step benches and other fascinating equipment. To participate in most of these activities, one needed arms and hands. I would have particularly liked to do the 'flying butterfly' over the box, but had to content myself with watching the others. Perhaps I had to admit defeat in this area, but I encouraged myself by remembering that there was very little else which defeated me, and that I would be able to make up for lost time during the last thirty minutes of the evening. Five-a-side football took up this valuable last slot, and I needed no allowances made for this!

At first, though, the other boys were a little frightened to tackle me in case I fell over. They realised that when I fell, I usually cracked my head because I had no hands with which to cushion a fall. I soon taught them that I needed no special treatment, and before long was accepted as part of the team.

The Boys' Brigade is essentially a Christian organisation. I found, therefore, that the Christian input in our weekly meetings took on an importance similar to that which my friend Alan placed on it. He made it quite plain to all of us when he became a Christian and kept on about it ever afterwards! We all got heartily fed up with his talk of 'hell fire and brimstone'! He would openly pray for us all – and me in particular! I found it very irritating.

I would have liked to attend the Boys' Brigade church parades, however. I loved the uniforms and the sense of occasion, but most of the time I could not get transport to get me there. We had quite a lot of Christian input at school, one way and another. We had to attend church every Sunday; grace was always said before meals, and some of the staff would share bedtime prayers with us. I took it all for granted. It was just part of the everyday routine.

We were dependent on transport for a lot of the time at school, particularly during our time at Gardiner House. A journey to school one morning stands out in my mind for more than one reason. To begin with, it was the only occasion when the minibus had a punctured tyre. Our driver was not too happy about it, but we all thought it great fun! We chattered and laughed while poor Trevor, the driver, had to change the wheel. Eventually he finished the job and we piled on to the minibus again, knowing that we were now very late for school. We arrived at the end of morning assembly and I walked in just in time to be presented with the silver Woolworth's Achievement Cup for progress in all aspects of school life! It was a great moment, and one I remember with gratefulness and satisfaction.

In 1973 I had to move back to the Chalet so that I could have easier access to my Possum machine, each one having been built to serve the needs of an individual child. I was sad to leave Gardiner House and its 'out of school' feeling, but glad to be able to use the Possum because that meant I didn't have to use the arms. I quite enjoyed lessons so long as I did not have to wear arms, but for most of the time I was thwarted by the relentless struggle to make the arms work.

I loved our regular visits each Thursday to the public swimming-pool. I had learned to swim during a trip to Edinburgh, but my instructors now showed me how to develop dexterity and power in my legs. At this stage I had given up the 'doggy-paddle' for the more mature 'frog-kick'! The stretching exercises I practised in 'life skills' lessons helped a great deal, and I soon became proficient, gaining bronze, silver and gold medals for personal survival within a few years.

My friend George Cherry had occasion to be very glad I had been so conscientious in my swimming lessons when he inad-vertently took in a mouthful of water one day. I happened to be the only one who saw his distress as he began to sink. Somehow I managed to grab hold of him with my chin and shoulder, and dragged him to the side. A teacher then took over, and the gasping George recovered quickly. It was to be an incident that George would remember to this day.

By the time I was twelve, I had a new goal in mind. I wanted to be the first pupil from our school to swim sixty lengths of the pool – about one mile. I proudly read the report in the local paper in March 1974 which likened my success to an Olympic event, adding:

Not bad going for a twelve-year-old, but even more remarkable for a Thalidomide victim without arms. That's Brian – such a handicap fails to keep a good boy down in the water! What Brian misses with arm-power he makes up with strong, powerful legs, and when it comes to turning – no problem! He just dips his head like a duck and turns over. He is one of the forty disabled pupils at Fleming Fulton School who find new freedom in water. Naturally, Brian is the toast of the school at the moment. 'I doubt if any pupil here will repeat this,' said one member of staff, 'it's quite a feat for anyone.'

Last year he brought home two silver medals from the Junior Multi-Disabled Games at Stoke Mandeville, and today Brian is writing home to Mum and Dad with the news that he has achieved his final distance medal. 'This is as far as he can go,' explained his teacher.

Interestingly, during the following nine months, at least six others also accomplished their fifteen-hundred-metre certificates. One of these, Paul, born without arms or legs and with only vestigial feet, took three hours to complete the whole distance, receiving the loudest cheer on the final lap. I would like to think that my effort went some way to inspiring these others to equal my achievement. One mile did not mark the end of the line for me, however. I can now swim far further than that, and it is a sport I have enjoyed enormously over the years, together with table tennis and snooker.

I had something of a problem at first in discovering the best way of getting to grips with table tennis. I started by sitting on a high stool with the bat in between the biggest two toes of my left foot. Then I would swing my foot back in the hope of making a winning smash over the net but instead, I more often threw myself right off the stool! One day, however, I accidentally picked the bat up under my chin and against my right shoulder; then, tucking the handle under my collar for a much better grip, I realised I had found the answer. Now I could run after the wide-angled shots and have pretty good success. To serve, I threw the ball up with my foot and after much practice in getting the timing right, I could smash the ball over the net.

My friend George was ahead of me in snooker. He had a special metal weight made as a rest for his cue. It had two grooves, deep and shallow for different shots. I was so impressed with how George had mastered the game that I would often borrow his weighted rest. Standing on my right leg and lifting the left with the cue stick between my toes, I soon mastered it too.

The autumn term held a special attraction for us in that there were some very good horse chestnut trees in the school grounds. We would watch the trees and see how the conkers were coming along; then, some time in late October or early November, several of us would assemble complete with wheelchairs and crutches for the annual conker hunt.

My method of getting the conkers down from the trees was to fling one of my slippers up into the branches. Then, hopefully, my slipper would return, bringing a shower of conkers with it. Unfortunately, more than once my slipper did not return and it would take several other missiles to loosen its position and get it back down to me. It made no difference, however; up I would throw a slipper again and again. One day, with one slipper inevitably stuck in a particularly stubborn branch, I foolishly threw the other one up after it in the hope that they would both come down together. When they didn't, I was left with bare feet, and the rest of my friends helpless with laughter around me.

'Get a football,' I said with a spark of brilliance, 'that'll do the trick.'

Someone soon appeared with the football which I kicked

high into the tree after the slippers, but when this got stuck in the tree too, we all gave up. Later, it did not take the surprised caretaker long to work out why one of the trees was festooned with slippers and a football, and I was forced to explain to the Chalet staff why I returned slipperless. Since they were too high to be reached, I had to wait for the next very windy day to retrieve them, sopping wet from their perch.

Every six months or so a visit to the clinic at Edinburgh loomed, and I would have to go off for about a week to have the arms refitted or changed as I grew. With these visits continually coming round, I was supposed to show the doctors how much I had improved since the last visit. Most of the time, however, I did not improve. Neither did I *want* to improve. I wanted simply to be allowed to be myself and get on with my life without the encumbrance of artificial arms. Each time I had to wear them it reinforced the fact that I was not complete in other people's eyes. I apparently needed arms to make me acceptable. But I didn't *feel* incomplete. I felt like me. Couldn't they all see that I could do more or less everything anyone else could do? Did it matter that I did it with my toes instead of fingers?

I strove to increase my ability *without* the use of arms. Nothing stopped me from doing anything I wanted to do. I just found unique ways of doing it. While 'normal' people had to use their hands, I could do better! My toes, feet and legs were far more supple and mobile than those of 'normal' people. Couldn't they see and appreciate the fact that I was special in my own way? Why did everyone think I had to conform as nearly as possible to the common image? The visits to Edinburgh became the black spots of my years of childhood. They frustrated me, infuriated me, and left me cross and humiliated. On my return to school, I took out my anger on the other children and the staff.

'Come on, Brian,' said Miss Wells, 'it's good to see you back, but you must get on with your work – you've missed a lot while you were away.'

I fumed quietly. Why did I have to go away, then? I would be perfectly happy to remain at school and forget the arms forever. Work? How could I work wearing these arms? By the time I had worked out which muscle to flex in order to make the pencil move only to find the arm shoot off in another direction because I hadn't co-ordinated some other part of my body, I would have forgotten what I wanted to write! Take off these horrible arms and leave me alone and I could do my work, I raged. If my friends spoke to me I would grunt back or shout at them. I felt cross, miserable and defeated.

I did not know it at the time, but someone else appreciated my point of view. Mrs Ferguson, the senior school child-care assistant, could see what we were going through. She saw that I was not the only one who hated prostheses. Almost all the other children felt the same way. It didn't seem to matter whether they were false arms or legs; they were all extremely difficult to use and made us feel more alienated.

We all suffered from sores and bruises where they rubbed against our skin, and almost without exception we longed to give them up for good. I also found out later that in Mrs Ferguson's opinion, the doctors could only see their wonderful, expensive inventions – they did not see the children who struggled to make sense of them. They persuaded and cajoled the children to use them – after all, a fortune had been spent on development, and didn't they have the potential to impart 'normality' to 'incomplete' children? Surely, they thought, children were self-conscious without arms or legs. They needed these wonderful inventions to help them come to terms with their disabilities.

Rather, we were self-conscious when we were *wearing* the prostheses – not when we were free of them. Left alone, most of us coped extremely well. With prostheses we were reduced to feelings of inferiority and helplessness. I felt that I could never be happy and content with life if I had to constantly wear arms. Depression set in and I became morose and withdrawn.

6

Holidays

Most of the time, terms at school were judged by how long it would be until the next holiday and I could go home. One never knew – *this* might just be the holiday when my mother would accept me as I was and refuse to send me back to Fleming Fulton. Not that school was all that bad. It just represented the fact that I needed to be altered to become acceptable to the world in general and my parents in particular. As the end of term drew near, so my spirits rose and I counted the days to the holiday.

I soon discovered, however, that half-term holidays didn't count. Apart from the expense of the air fare, it was considered that in my emotional state it would be unwise to allow me to go home for short lengths of time. They decided it would unsettle me too much and it would be far better to make arrangements for me to stay with a family close by. So when half-term arrived and all the other children and staff went off joyfully to their homes, I, alone, had to go to stay in the home of strangers. It hurt me badly, and reinforced my feelings of rejection.

Once I got used to the idea, staying in different homes had its advantages. First, my stay was usually short enough for my hosts to spoil me completely! My diet would always be the first thing to go – my hosts could not be expected to cater for special diets, although they were always given comprehensive details of my needs. So I revelled in the kind of foods that I had missed – sweets, puddings and mountains of home-cooked delicacies.

I stayed in a variety of homes, usually that of one of my friends, but sometimes in the home of teachers, which in spite of some apprehension on my part, turned out to be great fun. I slept in a variety of places: in a converted barn, in a tent in the garden and in an attic; and *on* a diversity of beds – the floor, an air-bed, a settee and a bunk bed. I learned to sleep well on anything!

I particularly enjoyed staying with Mrs Thompson, my physio-therapist. With three children of her own, she certainly knew how to make me welcome. A stay with the Thompson family was always good for a lot of fun and games. Mr Thompson ran a Saab garage, and often took us all out in his own Saab – a wonderfully powerful car that impressed me no end!

One half-term holiday proved especially difficult for the staff to place me because I was confined to a wheelchair. I had torn the ligaments in my right ankle after a bad fall doing a 180-degree turn while playing football, and my leg was encased in plaster. It must have been considered too much to expect any of my usual hosts to grapple with me and my wheelchair, so Mr and Mrs Thompson willingly took me in. If I had had normal arms, I could have used crutches – and these would have been difficult enough to handle – but since crutches were out of the question, I had to be ferried around in my chair. This did not suit me, of course, and since I kept on getting out of it to walk instead of waiting for someone to push me, I had to submit to three separate remoulding sessions on my heel. Mrs Thompson nobly took on the responsibility of trying to keep me in my chair.

It must have been quite a sacrifice for her and her husband, since I arrived at a time when they were redecorating their house. I simply could not sit by and see everyone else involved in all the activity, so Mrs Thompson took a deep (silent) breath and gave me a paint-brush to hold in the toes of my left foot and allowed me to paint the skirting-board! The result looked all right to me, but I don't know what they really thought of it!

Over the years there must have been fifty or sixty short holidays when I stayed in various homes. None of them took the place of my own home, but they certainly did their best to entertain and look after me. I was introduced to hundreds of different people from my hosts' circles of friends, and taken to all sorts of entertainments: bingo clubs, social clubs, sports clubs, and one pub. In fact, I actually stayed at the pub. It belonged to the father of a thalidomide friend of mine, Oliver, who always seemed to have a story to tell. I found out why in the course of my being introduced to many of the regular customers. They were all Irish, of course, and naturally full of Irish blarney!

Sometimes I stayed with my friend David Loughran and his family. I loved these times particularly since we got on so well together. A thalidomide like me, David's artificial arms had a very life-like hand which pushed into a socket at the end of one of the arms. One day we accompanied his mum to do the shopping, and stopped at the greengrocer's. David prodded around the cauliflowers with his false arm and hand while his mum went in to give her order. Soon the assistant came out to pick a cauliflower, but somehow David did not realise that he had left his hand among them. When the girl picked up the cauliflower, there beneath was a disembodied hand! The poor girl went white and panicked, screaming and shaking with shock! David, his mum and I were in stitches of laughter as they shoved the false hand back in its socket!

Three times in each year I went home to the Isle of Man. How I looked forward to the two weeks at Christmas and Easter, and the seemingly endless nine weeks of the summer holiday. Once at home, artificial arms could be forgotten. I think my mother couldn't bring herself to insist on my wearing them, knowing that I had to submit to them all through the school term, so I knew I could get them out of my sight for the length of the holiday. But I had to wear them for the journeys to and from home. On the one hand it seemed little enough to suffer before setting them aside for the whole holiday, but I could expect that the journey – even though only from Belfast to Ronaldsway – would often be gruelling. The flights seemed to be prone to delays because of fog either at Ronaldsway or at Belfast (maybe as a result of being near Lough Neagh, the largest natural lake in the British Isles). Either way, it meant that I would be stuck with the arms on for up to eight hours at a time. Throughout all the years I had been made to wear them, I never got used to them and they always caused me pain both physically and emotionally. By the time I got to the end of the journey I would be totally exhausted. The only occasional lifting of the gloom was to be asked sometimes to go up into the cockpit and see the pilot and the aeroplane controls. I loved this and could not fail to be amazed by all the levers and dials.

One trip home for Christmas proved to be the most frightening I have ever had. I was a seasoned traveller after a few years, but on this occasion I had to take a seat on a small postal plane which had places down one side for a few people only. I found this uncomfortable enough, but add to it the worst turbulence I ever experienced, and the result was that I really learned to pray that day! The little plane lurched up and down at an alarming rate, and I think I may have been too frightened even to feel sick!

Once at home, I quickly rammed the arms in a cupboard and savoured my freedom. Now I could show my parents and the rest of the family just how well I could cope with anything and everything. Perhaps Mum would realise at last that I managed far better without arms.

I showed how I could turn pages of my books extremely accurately, turn light switches on and off, and even reach up to peg clothes on a line. I put money into a telephone box and dialled with my big toe while standing on one leg, and I held the receiver under my chin. I could grip anything between my chin and the top of my shoulder, including cricket and table tennis bats, golf clubs (when I 'caddied' for my brother Alan), and I could even carry a chair to the table. I kept coins in a pocket at the bottom of my trouser leg or in my left shoe. (Only my *left* shoe – strangely, coins kept here are comfortable, but anything in my right shoe is far from comfortable!)

I cut things with foot-operated scissors which were invented by Trevor Baylis OBE, the inventor who brought the clockwork radio to the world market. He had focused on gadgets for the disabled for many years, and the scissors proved a great advantage to those of us without arms.

I had learned to hold a cup by linking the handle between my two largest toes. At the start, I tipped many a cupful of hot tea all over the floor, but I soon developed the dexterity to hold it firmly. It was an infinitely safer way of handling a cup than to hold it with the hook of the arms. The contrary hook would open at the most unfortunate moments and I despaired of ever being able to drink anything using them.

From a very young age I never had any intention of being left out of any games that my brother and sisters and school-friends played. My mother feared for my safety, and warned them to be careful what they did, and to look after me, but I had no fears, and followed wherever they led. My brother and sisters were my first role models, of course, but it was only in later years that I realised the part their help and encouragement played in my development. I could never sit and be simply a spectator in their games. I wanted to join in.

My limitations existed only in the length of time it took me to work out how I could copy them, but they accommodated me sometimes by varying the rules. The first time I played rounders with them, they opted to use a tennis ball. This helped a little, and I managed to hold the bat between my toes. It did not come easily to start with, however. I often missed the ball, but when I let go of the bat, sometimes it flew out at an angle and hit one of the other kids. Although amazingly patient with me, their charity became stretched to the limit as the game had to be halted time and time again, so that I could be given another try or to pacify a bruised child. I persevered, not wanting to be left out, but sometimes my toes blistered and bled with the effort, and then no one wanted Brian on their team.

My brother, Alan, suggested a change in the rules which might save everyone's temper. 'Why don't you simply kick the ball with your left foot instead of using the bat?' he asked, knowing that my left leg has always been the strongest. 'Then, when you're "fielding", if you head the ball we'll take that as a catch.'

This was a wonderful idea. Now I could really enter into the game. When my turn came round, I hit the ball with my left foot so hard that it shot high into the air and came down in the next field.

'That's not fair!' shouted the other team. 'It's not fair – you having Brian in your team!'

With a little assistance from the other children, or with some improvisation on my part, I always managed to join in most things, so that I would not be left out. I had to help with the chores, too. All the family had daily jobs to do in the guest-house. With up to sixty-five guests, Mum would have to get up at 5.30 a.m. to prepare the full English breakfasts, and then with Dad she would prepare the lunch. Alan had to clean and peel the potatoes in the potato machine, while Pat made the desserts and waited at tables with Gwen. My tasks were to empty all the wastepaper bins; empty and clean the ash-trays and take piles of old newspapers down to the main bin in the yard. In the evenings there would invariably be arguments when the girls wanted to go out with their friends, but had to stay to help.

Saturdays were particularly busy because most guests left and a new lot came in, and all the bed-linen had to be changed. This was my job, too. I would strip the beds and roll the sheets along the landings to the bathrooms where I had to get into the bath and tread the sheets for twenty minutes to give them a good soaking. It was a bit like grape treading, only with filthy linen!

During the TT races fortnight in early June, (that is, the Tourist Trophy motorbike races) it seems as though the whole Island becomes a racetrack and every guest-house is packed. At these times the girls, Alan and I were banished to the attic rooms to sleep. I didn't like this very much because the stairs were very steep and without arms to steady myself, I found steep stairs quite difficult to negotiate – especially coming down. I suppose we made up for the inconvenience in the winter, however, when we could choose any room we liked to sleep in!

Another inconvenience affecting just me was the fact that whenever I came home to the Isle of Man I seemed to develop an asthmatic wheeze. For some reason it never affected me in Belfast, but at home I often found it particularly difficult to breathe easily at night. Mum would come and prop a pillow under my head and give me a cuddle. When I returned to school, though, the asthma would amazingly clear up after a few days. Thankfully, I gradually improved as I grew older and it hardly worries me at all now.

During the summer holidays Mum would have no trouble fattening me up ready for the return to school. With all the guests to cater for, there was always plenty of food, so she indulged me with my special favourites of fried potato and onions. I never had to ask for puddings – there were plenty of yummy ones prepared for the guests every day. I particularly loved peppermint Manx ice cream, and of course, she made sure a stock of maple syrup awaited my homecoming!

Being at home did not consist entirely of work, however. We still had lots of time to go out and play football or to play golf with my golf-mad brother, Alan. He had saved up all his paper-round money to buy a 7-iron and a putter, so we would head off to Onchan Park where there were 'pitch and put' greens. We would get there just after closing time so that Alan could practise his strokes. As a youngster, I used to run around in the semi-darkness searching for his golf balls!

After we arrived in the Isle of Man to live, it did not take Alan and me long to find a good place to play football. Port Jack Glen was just three minutes from our home. A beautifully kept glen with a narrow stream and a gravelled footpath on both sides, it was crossed by several stone footbridges. In spring the steep embankments would be covered in yellow and white daffodils among the shrubs. Needless to say, ball games were prohibited in the glen, but we disregarded this rule completely. Two bench seats were fixed to the ground on each bank, and these we used as goalposts. Our rules stated that the stream had to be jumped before shooting under the bench because that needed a little more skill to achieve. Mum was always baffled as to why I came home with soaking wet socks and trainers.

Port Jack Glen was also a real favourite with the local kids at night. Then we would play war games and hide-and-seek, hiding in the shrubs and undergrowth. We lost count of the number of occasions the gardener chased us out, and we would be really frightened, but it never stopped us from coming back to play again.

A little further away from our home was the Blackberry Lane Football Pitch. We could play happily here for hours, but more often than not we would launch into a game in the street. We all took turns at being goalkeeper – me too! A goalkeeper without arms! I was happy to slide around on the sand or grass, but I drew the line at diving for the ball in the road! Often I would take a header – literally – and fall flat on my face. Many a time I tottered home, half-concussed and with a very bloody nose which left a trail of blood behind me.

When I first came home to the Isle of Man on holiday, I became something of a novelty to the local children. In Ballyclare, everyone had known me from birth and accepted me without question, but here on the Island, the children looked puzzled.

'Where are your arms?' they would ask, and I would repeat for the umpteenth time that I was born without any.

'But why?' they would insist, and as an eight- or nine-year-old, I never found it easy to explain.

Living in a holiday resort, amusement arcades abounded, and all of them had notices outside which stated clearly: 'CHILDREN UNDER 18 YEARS NOT ALLOWED WITH-OUT AN ADULT'. This posed no problems for me, however. I could look remarkably innocent if I tried, and I turned this on as I walked into the arcades to watch the people play. Very often some of the winning pennies were left in the trays just waiting for me to come along, remove my shoe and scoop them out.

I managed to work out that some machines gave a better chance of winning, so I would watch the visitors play the machines, then when they gave up, I would go along, slip several pennies in – and hey presto! out would come fifteen! At times I had to limp home with forty to sixty pennies in my shoes! On the way I would drop into the newsagent's to buy sweets, ice cream and Coke drinks.

Another place we got to know and love was Port Jack Beach. My mates and I would descend the eighty steps to the shingle cove where we would play 'sinking ships'. This comprised throwing empty Coke tins into the sea and then sinking them by aiming pebbles.

After trial and error I learnt how best to balance the right kind of pebble on the top of my left foot, then swinging my leg back – not too far so the pebble would fall off – I aimed for the tin and swung my leg forward with all my might. It took a lot of practice, but I managed it pretty well in the end.

I also had to practise a lot to match the other kids at 'pebble skimming'. I held a flat, smooth pebble between my toes and got just the right angle to make it jump two or three times before sinking. Whatever the other children did, sooner or later I would do! Except for riding a bike. I would have loved to hurtle down the street with the wind whistling through my hair like the others, but I really had to accept that this was just too much for me. I regretted it badly, but I just had to accept the situation.

In July 1971, the Summerland Leisure Complex opened. Situated at the north end of Douglas seafront, its construction was described as 'a skin of plastic Oroglas', tinted bronze to give a natural light with the effect of golden sunrays. It was a spectacular building – bright and spacious and giving those inside the impression of having been transported to the Mediterranean. It held musical entertainment to suit every taste and had loads of activities and amusements. I spent a lot of my spare time there, getting in by using the complimentary tickets given to guest-houses, or by creeping in free through the back entrance beside the electric tram depot. Amazingly, up to ten thousand people could enjoy themselves within the centre at the same time, and with so much to see and do, they might return time and time again and still not exhaust all the possibilities.

I tried as many of the rides and amusements as I could, making my bottom sore with so many goes on the Big Slide; bouncing and somersaulting on the American Moon Walk and nearly making myself sick on the Caterpillar Roundabout! But on 2 August 1973, something happened which was to indelibly fix itself into the minds of all Manx people.

We had only recently moved to a guest-house about a mile from Summerland, and having finished their evening duties, my sister Pat and her friend Anne (who had been helping in the guest-house) decided to pop down to the amusement centre for an hour or so. At about eight o'clock a guest came rushing in to say that thick, black smoke was billowing from Summerland. This could only mean fire, and with horror I realised that Pat and Anne were there. Numb and shaking I ran off to find them, leaving Mum and Dad to follow behind. Sirens blazed and emergency vehicles raced from all directions to the scene, but my mind tumbled with thoughts of where Pat and Anne might be. They could be trapped inside one of the seven terraces or maybe down in the basement. How could I find them? Where could they be? I knew the complex well, but that only served to confuse me further. The girls might be anywhere. As I ran, through my mind flashed memories of the times I had gone to Sunday school as a small child. They told us that God was real and that he listened to our prayers – and even answered them. My friend Alan Wilson certainly believed that. He seemed to treat Jesus like a close friend. With this raging inferno ahead of me, it would seem that only God could deliver my sister and her friend if they were still in there. I could do no more than murmur, 'God, keep them safe.' I didn't know whether this was a 'proper' prayer or not.

Of course, I could do nothing except stand back and watch and wait in horror like everyone else as the inferno raged, but I cannot describe my relief when Dad pushed through the crowds to tell me that the girls had got out safely. They must have passed by me in the frantic crowds running from the scene, but had been seen by Mum and Dad. They were shaken and badly frightened, but otherwise unhurt. It would, however, take them a long time to get over the experience.

We heard the next day that the entire complex had been gutted and that fifty people had died in the catastrophe. Many more had been injured both physically and emotionally, and even Pat and Anne suffered bouts of tearfulness for some time afterwards. The papers reported that the fire had been started by youths playing with matches, and the plastic Oroglas covering ignited immediately. It took only twenty minutes for the whole complex to be ablaze.

I had no idea whether my hasty prayer had been instrumental in securing Pat and Anne's safety, but I found myself taking a little more interest when my friend Alan, back at school, talked to me about God.

As the day approached for me to return to Belfast, I became increasingly despondent. School loomed over me like a huge black cloud darkening the last few days of my holiday. I became irritable and moody, and shed many tears on my pillow each night.

To add to my burden, the arms had to be retrieved from their cupboard, ready for the journey back. Since Mum had fed me up during my stay, getting the arms on was always a struggle. Mum pushed and pulled and stretched the straps over my expanded waistline, adding to the general discomfort, but I reckoned that it was worth it for all the lovely food I had enjoyed. Once back at school I settled into the routine, but more often than not weekends were the times when I would pine for my family – especially when writing letters home on Sunday afternoons.

I drifted into joining in some of the Christian activities in which my friend Alan took part. Two of the staff led a Bible study on Tuesday nights and I started going along. There were only about five or six of us, but I gradually began to understand what Alan had been talking about for so long.

Then one evening a member of staff made arrangements for a group of us to see the film *A Thief in the Night*, made by the Billy Graham Association. It attempted to portray the cataclysmic events that will happen in the last days of this age, according to biblical prophecy. It pulled no punches and terrified us all. But the message was clear: God would one day judge the sinful world, but all who believe that Jesus Christ died to take the punishment for sin would be saved from God's judgment.

Then there were our Saturday evening visits to 'the Centre', in Newcastle, County Down, where the preacher Derick Bingham spoke. He became a good friend to us all at the Chalet. The songs and hymns we sang reminded me of my Sunday school days, and I joined in eagerly. There were many new songs being written at that time with easily understood words, and although I liked the old hymns, the new ones were a refreshing change. Our favourite, by Gloria and William Gaither, embodied the Christian faith in a verse:

Because he lives, I can face tomorrow,
Because he lives all fear is gone,
Because I know he holds the future
And life is worth the living just because he lives.

As I sang these words all the teaching I had heard over the years from Sunday school to Boys' Brigade seemed to come together. The joy of knowing that Christ had conquered death and that because of it I didn't need to have a fear of the future seeped into my mind and solidified into a wonderful revelation. It was all true! I believed it! And I knew that because I believed, I too was saved from God's judgment. I would be safe in Christ both now and in the future and for eternity. What a wonderful truth!

Now I looked at my friend Alan in a different light. I understood what he and my Christian teachers – several of whom had faithfully tried to lead us into knowledge of Christ – had been trying to tell me. Nothing could be more important. From now on my life would have a different impetus as I lived knowing that Christ was in me and with me.

7

Free at last!

I was not aware that several members of staff had been questioning the usefulness of artificial limbs. As far as I knew, all the adults around me had with one accord determined that my future would best be served by becoming proficient with false arms, and no one seemed to be listening to my side of the problem. I lived in the continual frustration of knowing that I could do better and achieve more *without* arms, but it seemed that only I held that opinion.

However, the tantrums and suffering of those of us who had to struggle daily to use artificial arms and legs had not gone unnoticed. Some of the staff had been suffering with us as they saw our distress and tried to encourage us to keep on trying. We could not know that over a long period of time our plight had been discussed and argued, and that all the deliberations were coming to fruition.

Our occupational therapist hung out for one last try. 'The seniors may have better control with the limbs. Let them persevere a little longer for just a few hours each day –

I'm sure they would benefit from their use.'

But I, at least, was old enough now to complain for myself. At thirteen years of age I had enough experience to know that I could do almost anything better without false limbs. I did not want to conform to other people's ideas of how I should look. I wanted to be myself and to be allowed to get on with my life in my own way. I fought every attempt to strap me into the harness and showed just how well I could manage my schoolwork if left to get on with it without these added incumbrances.

At last I put my foot down. 'I *will not* wear these awful arms again,' I declared. 'I can do anything and everything much better without them. What's the point? They only slow me down and make me furious. Please let me do things my own way. I don't need artificial arms.'

To my surprise, my complaints were finally heard. The momentous decision broke on my unbelieving consciousness. 'All right, Brian, we'll give in. We think you've tried them long enough. They certainly don't seem to be working for you. From now on you can concentrate on improving your technique with your toes.'

I was ecstatic! Could my struggle really be over? After eleven years of trying to be someone else's idea of what I ought to be, could I now relax and be myself at last? I looked at the revolting contraptions lying on the floor. Hateful things! My father had been right all along. He had told my mother that I didn't need artificial arms and he was right! I know Mum wanted me to have the best chance, but in this instance my best chance meant leaving me to be myself. I would have liked a grand destruction ceremony to get rid of the arms once and for all, but I simply contented myself with my new freedom. At last the glorious day had come! The hideous arms were banished forever! Now I could live properly. I could be the Brian I had known all along that I could be.

Some time later I discovered that almost all children without arms or legs discarded their prostheses eventually. The success rate of these very expensive inventions turned out to be very low. Dr Vaughan of Guy's Hospital, London, wrote in *The Sunday Times*:

> Limbless children were fitted with artificial arms and legs in the hope that modern engineering ingenuity could give them back some of the functions the drug Thalidomide had stolen from them. But engineers are no match for Nature. Sometimes all that the metal legs and unwieldy arms could do was to give the wearer some outward appearance of normality. At least he/she was the right shape.
>
> Inwardly, the picture was very different. In many cases, tiny deformed bodies had inelegant but potentially useful limbs amputated so that they could be strapped into the leather harness of the artificial legs or arms.

I agreed with him wholeheartedly. Artificial arms did nothing for me except make me look 'normal', but I wanted my own outline – and my outline did not include arms. I was Brian who happened to have no arms. I was not incapable or dependent. I could manage perfectly well without arms. At last I could prove it!

Now began a time of challenge. I could get on with my schoolwork without encumbrances. Not that everything suddenly became easy – it didn't. New problems presented themselves daily and I had to find ways to overcome them. 'If at first you don't succeed, try, try again' became my motto, and try I did. I would persevere until perspiration poured down my face and I became exhausted with effort. But I would not give up. I passed through various intensities of all emotions: frustration, anger, despair, relief, until at last, I succeeded. Then joy and elation took over. The satisfaction of achievement would lead me on to the next challenge. I would not be stopped by anything!

I had a lot of schoolwork to catch up on. The years of struggle with arms had left me way behind in my studies. Now I had to make up the time. I worked hard and with much more interest now that I didn't have to concentrate on making the arms work. I began to enjoy my work and get on with it eagerly.

My last few years at school were much more satisfying than the previous years as I studied for my O-levels, taking maths, English language and English literature. I used the Possum most of the time for writing, getting up a good speed. The numbers representing the letters soon disappeared in my mind and I was able to 'think' letters and so write more effectively.

Matters at home changed yet again – but only briefly. During the summers of 1975 and 1976, Dad apparently still had 'itchy feet', and Mum wrote to tell me that they were all moving – this time to Blackpool! My initial thoughts were that they would all be even further away than on the Isle of Man, but I rationalised the thought by telling myself that it really wasn't much further, and that holidays would be good fun, anyway!

They took a guest-house just off the Central Promenade and Central Pier, and when my long summer holiday arrived I relished the seven miles of beaches and the long Golden Mile with its tantalising amusement arcades. I marvelled at Blackpool Tower and tried out rides in the Pleasure Park, although I found some of them just too scary to risk without arms to hang on with.

I can't say that I was particularly disappointed, however – or even surprised – to hear only a year later that Dad was planning to take the family back to the Isle of Man. The Island had captivated him back in the 1960s, and everything else seemed to take second place. Perhaps it had been more of a surprise that he had tried the mainland experiment in the first place.

I achieved another first at about this time – albeit a small one. I had always longed to ride a bicycle, but without arms to hang on with, it proved just too dangerous. But when a cycle-hire shop opened on the central promenade in Douglas, I noticed that tandem cycles were on offer. These were a variety of tandem on which two people could sit side by side. What a thrill it was for me, therefore, to sit next to my sister Pat, pedalling for all we were worth along the two-mile length of the seafront with the wind flying through our hair! At last I knew what it was like to ride a bike!

When I was sixteen, I had the opportunity to travel abroad for the first time. The Thalidomide Trust arranged a trip to Sorrento, Italy, for fifteen thalidomides with eight helpers and friends. For two weeks we stayed in the luxury of the Grand Hotel with opulence greater than I had ever experienced before, with superb rooms and amenities, including a lift from our cliff-top perch down to the beach below.

On one particular evening we all went to a disco on the Piazza Tosso. I had been quite sheltered up to this time, hardly ever having drunk alcohol. Everyone was drinking the local beer so I felt obliged to join in, but as the glasses did not have handles, I drank through a straw and several others joined me. After three or four pints of the lethal brew I threw myself rather too whole-heartedly into the disco dancing, but worse, I awoke the next morning with a hangover! I resolved that this should be the first and last time such a thing would happen and I have kept my word ever since. Alcohol is not for me!

During the stay we made a wonderful trip to Rome which

left me speechless at the beauty of St Peter's and the Sistine Chapel, although I have to admit to conflicting thoughts about the poverty of the first Peter, with the unimaginable opulence of the church dedicated to him. It was a wonderful trip full of marvellous things to do and see, and I shall always be grateful for the opportunity to experience it all – especially in such luxury.

Back at school in the same year, I was made a prefect with my friend George Cherry as head boy. We were allowed various privileges with these positions, together with a change of tie colour to denote our rank. It was all a great honour and we responded positively. The trust and authority invested in us gave a boost to our self-esteem, and we tried to fulfil our duties faithfully.

At the end of 1978 I was gratified to discover that I had gained O-levels in maths, English language and English literature, and went on to Hereward Sixth Form College, Coventry, on the mainland, for another year in order to take more O-levels.

My year at sixth-form college proved eventful. I discovered that the Thalidomide Trust, set up to help and monitor the progress of the victims, had a major objective. They aimed that every victim should, as far as possible, be able to have full mobility in the use of a car. From the main funds, a specially adapted car would be provided, together with driving lessons. I heard, therefore, shortly after my seventeenth birthday, that a Mini car would be delivered to me in early December, from the workshops near Heathrow Airport where it had been adapted for my use. I awaited its arrival with the greatest excitement, and when the day finally came I was thrilled to be given a 'tour' of its features.

The car was equipped so that I could handle all the controls with my feet. It had automatic gears, and a steering disc on the floor. My left foot steered and manipulated the 'hand' brake lever, while my right foot was kept busy with the brake pad, the lights, wipers, washers, horn, indicators and, of course, the accelerator.

Perhaps December was not a good time to be learning to drive because most of my lessons took place in heavy snow and ice! My instructor took it philosophically.

'If you are able to handle a car in this kind of weather, Brian, then you'll handle most eventualities in the future.'

I believed him eagerly, and went at my lessons confidently. I passed my test at the first attempt, and found myself mobile!

The end of this year brought more examinations, and to my great satisfaction I passed four more O-levels: in accountancy, commerce, economic history and geography. I was very pleased with this satisfactory end to my year's efforts, but now I had to consider what I would do next. I had to remember that I not only had to do as well as anyone with arms – I had to excel to be accepted.

The next step to my search for a career seemed to point in the direction of a course in business studies back home in the Isle of Man. To this end, therefore, I enrolled with the College of Further Education in Douglas for one more year of study.

At about this time, I began to take an increased interest in the trust fund that had been set up for me some years before. Ever since the thalidomide tragedy came to the public notice, sympathetic and involved parties had pursued a long fight for compensation. It took over ten years to come to fruition, but eventually the distributing company was forced to set aside a large amount of money to be held in trust for each of the victims. The resulting payment was not enough to allow us to be completely financially independent for the rest of our lives, but invested properly, it could help greatly towards our keep. I had nothing to do with my trust fund as a child, of course, as it was administered by a board of trustees until I reached the age of twenty-five, but I became increasingly eager to discover what was being done on my behalf.

I understood that the trustees held only a 'discretionary' portfolio, which meant that I could not interfere with the money, but I wanted to know how it had been invested and whether they were getting the best deals for me. At first, I revealed my eagerness to become involved by asking to attend the six-monthly meetings. As my first meeting drew near, I looked forward to finding out how they transacted the business and how I could play a fuller part in the proceedings. I therefore duly presented myself at the appropriate time and place to be greeted warmly by all the trustees.

As soon as I saw them all together in the one place, however, everything seemed far more intimidating than I had expected. Here was a group of experienced businessmen, dressed formally in the traditional dark suited 'uniform', relaxed and at ease in their own sphere of the imposing office suite. As the meeting got under way, I found myself submerged in a quagmire of baffling phrases and unknown jargon. I had no idea what they were talking about, and could only remain silent, feeling more like crawling under the table.

This would not do at all. I could not continue to be totally ignorant of matters that concerned my future. Something would have to be done about it. My college course already included studies regarding the importance of the City of London and the stock market for private and professional clients regarding investment decisions. I took a particular interest in the whole subject and then, to round it off, finally decided to take a correspondence course to study in depth the various possibilities of investing, so that I would be better equipped to understand the terms and jargon used by my trustees.

When I began the year's course, I was filled with enthusiasm and determined to excel at all the inevitable assignments. I had my Possum typewriter, which remained the fastest of my options for writing, but before long I began to run into difficulties. The Possum had taken quite a lot of punishment one way and another, with my toes pounding out words all day and every day, and now it began to protest. A highly specialised piece of equipment, local firms were simply not equipped to deal with its idiosyncrasies, and it became harder and harder to get it repaired.

With the Possum's increasing unreliability, I was thrown back into writing with my toes, and no matter how impressive it seemed to those who marvelled that I could write with my toes at all, it was still slower than a typewriter. I began to fall behind with my assignments.

I had formed a friendship with another student who had a different kind of problem, but found the going slow, just like me. Hammed Pishvie came from Iran, but was married to a Manx girl called Geraldine. A lively character, Hammed was as proud of his Iranian roots as I of my Ulster ones, and we shared many a joke together.

I spent many a happy evening at the home of Hammed and Geraldine, discussing topics which affected our different cultures, such as the importance of having a high esteem for family and parents, ethics and morality – all dear to the Iranian heart. Somehow, however, the conversation always drifted around to religion. I tried to share my little understanding of the Protestant and Roman Catholic history in Northern Ireland, and Hammed told of the Shia and Sunni of Iran, the seeming parallel being on-going conflicts.

At this particular time in my life I had 'shelved' God, yet talking to Hammed regarding the Quran and the Bible, I gradually began to realise how little substance and reality I had in my own faith in Christ since my schooldays. Looking back, I believe God was using Hammed to make me think about my position as a Christian, but I was still very reluctant to 'take the bait' and seek God afresh.

After a few months on the course, I had to be honest with myself and realise that even with the understanding and support of the tutors, I would not be able to keep up with the assignment projects. I did not find this easy to accept, but I am very grateful that I was allowed to continue to attend lectures and do selected essays until the end of the course. An added help was to be involved in group discussions regarding a wide range of subjects connected with business law, commerce, economics, investment and management structures without actually taking the examinations.

I left the college, disappointed that I did not have a diploma to prove my study, but at least I had gained a good ground knowledge of business matters and practice. Could the time be right for me to step out on my own in business?

For some time I had been nurturing aspirations of starting some form of mail-order business and I mentioned this to Hammed. He seemed enthusiastic, but extended my outline ideas. Hammed had an incredible way of convincing others that they needed just what he had to offer. He had a very impressive and persuasive manner and obviously felt he could add something to any enterprise.

'What about going into business together?' he enthused. He enlarged on this by suggesting that his gifts would lend themselves to taking a more direct role on the selling side of the business, and that I could perhaps be a 'sleeping partner' by mainly supplying the finance.

Hammed's interests lay in the importing of delicacies and speciality goods from the East, such as Persian carpets, caviare and other exotic products. It sounded good to me, and so we began a partnership, grandly calling ourselves the 'Hambry Import and Export Company'.

Our joint enterprise lasted just about eight months. In that time we both realised how different we were regarding business in values, ambitions and risk factors. We could not continue to work at odds with one another, so decided to part amicably and go our separate ways. Now the time had come for me to test the market and look for full-time paid work.

8

Self-sufficient!

In spite of the setback in my education until the age of thirteen through being compelled to concentrate on using arms instead of studying, in just four or five years I felt I had equipped myself reasonably well. I now had seven good O-levels, each of which provided a sound foundation for work, and I had a good knowledge of business studies, even if I did not have the diploma as evidence of it. I now had to prove my parents and everyone else wrong in their conviction that I would need arms before I could be employable.

I was not naïve enough to think that finding a job would be simple, for I fully realised that in most people's eyes I was 'disabled'. That I could do pretty well everything anyone else could do – given just a little consideration to my method of doing it – did not seem to come into the equation. I knew most people would think I *looked* wrong, therefore I must be incapable. But I had done my homework in more ways than one. From my studies in business law at college, I knew something of the rights and obligations of employers with regard to giving disabled people equal opportunities to work. The Disabled Persons Employment Act, 1946 stated that 3 per cent of a workforce of twenty employees and over of any employer in the Isle of Man should be disabled. With this legislation, I felt there ought to be a good chance for me to find work somewhere.

During the following four months I discovered the huge chasm between government legislation and reality in the workplace. I did not believe that I had a right to walk into a job without appropriate training or qualifications simply because I could be labelled 'disabled', but I did not apply for any post which I felt I would not have a reasonable chance of getting.

Fact seemed miles away from reality, however. Time and again I came away from interviews very hurt by the repeatedly offered frivolous or lame excuses as to why I could not be employed. I was told that 'company image' would be at stake or the office layout did not lend itself to my particular difficulties; they were sometimes sure that I 'would not be able to keep up the pace', and even – 'off the record' of course – 'we prefer not to have the hassle'.

I glanced through the pile of rejection letters I had received. All the petty excuses cloaked one real phrase. They said, 'Brian, you are unemployable.' Again and again I saw it behind the forced politeness: 'You are unemployable. You are unemployable.'

In despair I found myself forced to the conclusion that the odds were stacked against me, even in a time of comparatively high employment. The resulting knocks to my ego left me low and discouraged, with the feeling that all my struggles to come to terms with my lack of arms counted for nothing. I remained an outcast and socially isolated. I thought back on my mother's warnings and fears over the years of my childhood.

'What will become of you?' she had said when I refused to wear the horrible arms. 'How will you ever earn your living without arms?' she had insisted, holding the tortuous harness ready for me to put on, while I resolutely glowered back at her. 'Try, Brian,' she would coax. 'You need arms to get on in the world.'

Had she been right? Did I really need to *look* right before anyone would begin to take me seriously? But *those* arms. I pictured them. Horrible, ugly lumps of metal and plastic which took me all my time to think into moving where I wanted them to go. Surely they could not be the answer to my employability? Could it really be that if I had persevered with them after all, an employer would look more favourably on me?

I seriously doubted whether they would have made any real difference to the situation, and anyway, I had not persevered with them, and I was glad I hadn't. They would certainly not have helped me to become proficient in anything. They were too difficult to handle. I began to see things more clearly. I could not do half the things I did now if I had to do them with arms. They simply hampered and restricted my actions.

I reminded myself that I had never been a quitter. 'Try, try, try again,' my parents, teachers and friends had drummed into me whenever I got stuck. I had not been defeated at anything for long. Persistence always won in the end. But would persistence win in the real world? How many jobs did I have to apply for before I would be forced to admit defeat?

It had been four or five years since I had given my life to the Lord Jesus Christ as a thirteen-year-old. During those early days of being a Christian I learned how God cares for his children and has a plan for their lives. 'Nothing happens to a child of God by chance or accident,' I was taught. 'And we know that in all things God works for the good of those who love him, who have been called according to his purpose' (Romans 8:28), my Boys' Brigade leader told us.

But I had grown up now. I had left my childish faith for adult beliefs. God did not seem as close as he had in those childhood days. What difference could a belief in God make now in my desperate situation? Could he save me from becoming a useless drain on the state simply because no one would believe I could do as well as someone with arms?

I had almost given up searching the 'situations vacant' columns. It hardly seemed worth the trouble. But my dad had not given up. One evening he spoke from behind the pages of the local newspaper. 'What about trying the civil service, Brian?'

I frowned, but listened.

'There are two positions advertised here. One requires book-keeping skills, and the other needs a statistician.'

I had no doubts that I had the skills to at least make a go of either post, but would it be another 'wild goose chase' resulting in disappointment and humiliation? I attended for interview a week or two later, full of nerves and not a little distrust. Mr Harold Moore, the Chief Executive of the Isle of Man Government Harbour Board, made me surprisingly welcome. I was not used to the feeling it gave me when he appeared pleased to see me. More than that, he seemed to positively *care*. He called for coffee, and we sat down to discuss the position. I slipped my foot from my shoe and swung it over my other leg ready to pick up the coffee cup with my toes. At any other time it would be an involuntary movement, but today I felt completely self-conscious. I reminded myself to grip the handle carefully and to hold the cup steady. I did not want to spoil everything by spilling the coffee on the floor. Had I missed anything Mr Moore had said while I had been thinking what I was doing?

'Brian, we are looking for someone who is good with statistics.'

I assured him that I felt this was within my capabilities, and told him briefly about my training.

'If we were to take you on,' went on Mr Moore, 'what assistance or practical help would you need?'

I smiled. This was quite a different type of interview from any I had previously experienced. All the others could only see difficulties and problems before they happened. This employer seemed prepared to give a little if necessary. I would prove to him that virtually nothing was necessary. I showed him how I wrote with my toes; how I could turn pages of books, work the computer and use a calculator. The only concession I requested was the use of a decent bit of floor space – preferably with a carpet – where I could sprawl out with all my books and equipment. I could use a desk, but it was easier for me to sit on the floor rather than perching on a stool or chair – and anyway, things didn't fall off the floor! In fact, I could make a good case for anyone – with or without arms – using the floor instead of the restriction of a desktop!

'Right, Brian,' Mr Moore said resolutely, 'I'll give you a three-month trial period. We'll see how you get on. How will that do?'

I was completely astonished. In fact, I wondered if my ears were giving me one of their occasional bouts of trouble. Did I really hear Mr Moore offering me a job? He grinned at my obviously thunderstruck look. I left the interview on cloud nine. What a wonderful boost it gave to my self-esteem. Someone really wanted me to work for him! I was employed! I had paid work and could now be self-sufficient!

I duly presented myself for duty the following Monday, and set about proving my worth. My office was situated in the main Douglas Sea Terminal building, with beautiful panoramic views across Douglas Bay and the rolling hills as a backdrop from my window. I could see all the activity in the harbour area, although positioning myself on the floor below window level, I could not be distracted by outside events. Here I got to grips with the job, working furiously each day, stopping only for the occasional coffee or tea break, and clearing up my widely spread papers before going home so as to leave the floor clear for the cleaners.

I knew I was 'on trial'. I had to compare favourably with my able-bodied colleagues, competing with them on equal terms. No favours were given or wanted. I would be as useful as any of them – no, I would be *more* useful. They had to see and understand that a lack of arms did not affect my brain or my ability to succeed in the workplace. Consequently I worked longer, harder and quicker than anybody else did.

'For goodness sake, slow down!' I was told. 'You'll run us all into the ground!'

I grinned back in satisfaction. Now they knew what could be done.

After a few months, Harold Moore offered me my own office. Now I could spread everything out across the floor all the week until Friday, when I would have a grand tidying session. I joked that all my colleagues would have to get on their knees when they came to see me now! I did have a desk to make it easier to present papers and discuss with colleagues and visitors, but before long one of the engineers in another department suggested an improvement to my comfort.

'What about sawing off the stem of that swivel-chair so you will be nearer the floor to work?' he said. 'You might find it easier to move your legs about.'

No sooner said than done, my chair was returned to me

without its stem so that I could position myself about four inches from floor level. And so I contentedly began my working life in full-time, paid employment.

My job description entailed doing ledger bookkeeping, compiling reports for the various sections of the department – in particular for the represented members of the House of Keys, the Isle of Man Government, regarding financial costings related to the harbours of the Island. I enjoyed working very much as part of a team, fitting myself into the scheme of things and preparing for a long, satisfying stay. I did not intend to seek promotion within the civil service. I had no aspirations for greater responsibility. I merely hoped to remain with the Harbour Board for a few years and then, when I had accumulated enough capital, perhaps establish myself with my own business, possibly with a friend.

During these early years at the Harbour Board, I took to popping into the newsagent's each morning on my way to work to buy a copy of the *Financial Times* and the *Daily Mail*. I kept the coins in my left shoe, so would slip my foot out, pick out the coins with my toes and pass them to the assistant. Then, with the two papers tucked under my chin, I headed off to the office.

My portfolio of stocks and shares were reviewed by my trustees every six months, but I could not just sit back and let them get on with it. I wanted to become personally involved in the decision-making and be more responsible for my own future. I reckoned that with my recently acquired expertise, I could possibly equal my trustees' knowledge of the market but, more significantly, I suspected that financial opportunities were being missed. Perhaps I was a little arrogant, but I did not feel I argued from a position of complete ignorance. I would pore through the stocks and shares pages of the *Financial Times*, familiarising myself with their ups and downs.

'Got any good tips?' quipped Harold, as he passed my door and saw me engrossed in my *FT* over my cup of coffee.

I grinned. As yet I was merely a beginner trying to find 'the lie of the land', but as I continued to study the markets and apply my knowledge, I began to doubt the value of stocks and shares for my purposes. It seemed to me that property would make a better investment, and to this end I began to pester my trustees.

Since I had another five years to go before I could take control of the trust fund, I would need the consent of the trustees before I could effect any changes to the situation. My parents, therefore, as my closest trustees, were the first to hear my ideas.

'Look, Dad,' I argued, 'you know what the market is like in holiday flats, don't you?' Dad's speculations with guest-houses and holiday flats had proved financially sound and I knew he could not counter my arguments. 'Stocks and shares are always risky, but property is undoubtedly the safest investment. If I had property of my own, my investment would be as safe as possible. I'm sure that's true, isn't it?'

I did not add that it would also mean that I would have a greater control of my own affairs, but this, too, was my great aim. Indeed, Dad could not argue with me. He was inclined to think me right, but the experienced businessmen handling my affairs would have to be convinced too. It might not be so easy to change their minds.

It took about fifteen months of hard discussions to effect the change, but eventually my wishes were cautiously accepted, and I was allowed to begin looking for appropriate property. And so for some time afterwards, a continual stream of estate agents beat a path to my door with large bundles of papers under their arms.

The properties ranged from offices, retail premises and industrial units to apartments or flats. I fairly quickly eliminated most of the options, leaving the flats and holiday apartments. I had some knowledge of these through Dad's experience. But then the viewing began.

What a wide range of conditions I found! Some were so dilapidated that it would take a fortune to put them back into order, but many were very good. I needed to eliminate further and fine-tune my needs to decide exactly what would suit my situation.

I decided that the properties should be in the Douglas or Onchan areas, so that I could oversee them more easily. I tried to be businesslike and sensible about the whole thing, and determined not to rush into the first likely option. I took my time, gradually forming in my mind the kind of property I needed.

My search continued into a wet and blustery November in which an estate agent had shown me around several premises, none of which were suitable. I could argue that this time of the year would be the best time to view premises because one would see them at their worst. Viewing on a lovely sunny day when 'everything in the garden is lovely', might be more pleasant, but it does not show up the defects so well as a dreary downpour! So I took especial notice of the damp, any ventilation problems, and water supply, rather than being deceived by a lick of paint in the spring that could hide a multitude of problems. And then one day the estate agent rang me again.

'Brian, we've just got a property on our books which I think is what you are looking for. It's also in your price range.'

I had heard this line several times before so my expectations were not high, but I agreed to look it over. I met the estate agent at the address – a quiet garden square in the heart of Douglas. It looked pleasant and inviting on the crisp, bright and frosty morning, but I would not be taken in by outward appearances. I needed more assurance than that.

The building faced south and looked out over gardens belonging to the Douglas Corporation. It certainly had a very good aspect. It had been built in the 1880s as part of a four-storey-high terrace to provide holiday accommodation for the influx of summer visitors but Mrs King, the present owner, had remodelled the premises in the 1970s as permanent flats. She now intended to retire, and was looking for a buyer.

As I looked around the property, my toes checked everything: floorboards, switches, lights and behind the cupboards and wardrobes. I did not expect perfection, but I wanted to know what I was buying. Mrs King looked on in amazement as I prodded and poked, searched and inspected. She clearly had no idea that feet could be just as useful as hands!

With the inspection finished, I weighed up the possibilities. The building was in the right location, the right condition and it also had the right price tag. I reckoned I had discovered the right place at last. Now my trustees had to be approached.

I attended the next meeting with enthusiasm. I could not see any reason why they should object to my proposition. I presented my case, explaining in detail exactly what I saw as my priorities and how I felt this particular property fitted the bill. To my surprise and satisfaction, they agreed – on one condition. Until I reached the age of twenty-five, I must produce the certificate of insurance to be seen annually by the trustees. I agreed whole-heartedly. As trustees their duty was to protect my investment, and they could ask no less.

And so the block of flats in Hutchinson Square became mine. I savoured the independence it afforded me. At last I could be self-sufficient. I knew that some renovation and modernisation would be necessary as each flat became vacant, but I had allowed for this eventuality, and so could look forward to being a brand-new landlord and administering my own finances.

9

A new direction

I had budgeted for a lot of modernisation when I took on the flats, much of which would be needed to meet fire and health regulations, but it did not include paying professional decorators. In my usual fashion, I anticipated carrying out as much as possible myself, and for the rest I enlisted the help of my brother Alan.

Before long, therefore, the 'Gault team' could be found with radio echoing in the empty rooms while we happily got on with the work until late into the night. Our arrangement allowed for my territory to be anything below six feet in height with Alan taking the higher areas. I fixed the wallpaper stripper firmly between the toes of my left foot and worked energetically, while Alan whistled away merrily above me. I sandpapered and painted the skirting-boards, window sills and doors, with Alan doing the picture-rails and anything else above my height, and then the same arrangement continued for painting the walls.

It did not cause me any problems — although it might have done if we hadn't covered up all the furniture — I seemed to get more paint over myself and the floor than on the woodwork!

The paint roller proved most difficult for me to get to grips with, but I did not intend to let it beat me. I had to invest a bit of time in clearing up the spills before becoming really proficient as a decorator, but I managed it in the end. Seeing the smart, newly painted rooms gave me an enormous boost of confidence. Once again I had succeeded where some might assume I would fail. Brian could do anything if he kept on trying!

Some of the modernisation needed professional attention, however. Kitchens and bathrooms needed renewing, several fire doors had to be installed, and eleven windows had to be replaced. A variety of tradesmen were contacted and briefed in order to complete everything, and I delighted in dealing with them myself. I may have been quite young for a property owner, but I did not need anyone else to negotiate for me. I took my courage in both feet, as it were, and braved the stares of surprised strangers to explain what I needed, to acquire estimates and to get the work done. I learned to handle the initially startled reactions of people when confronted with a disability and who are momentarily put off. I made a point of putting them at their ease and alleviating their confusion – which all helped towards boosting my own confidence. I would be dependent on no one. Brian may have had no arms, but his brain remained intact and his abilities were as good as anyone with two arms. He did not need a 'minder'. He could cope with anything anyone else could do.

I found out on occasions that some of my prospective tenants needed to take in this fact, too. It amazed me that some people obviously held the subconscious view that disability affects the mind in some way. They seemed to think that because I lacked arms, I would therefore be a 'soft touch'. I suppose my youth had something to do with it, too, but I soon learned to become strict about my tenancy agreements. Most of those with whom

I dealt were very fair and understanding, but just occasionally one would try my patience and I had to deal firmly with the situation. It all went to help the young Brian towards maturity and I learned to take it all in my stride.

At last I felt I had control of my life. Everything had 'come together'. I had a good, satisfying job with the Harbour Board, but even more than this, as I took on tenants for the flats, I became financially independent. It did not all come easily, of course. I had to work hard to keep the flats in good condition, and I had to learn to deal with the occasional bad tenant, but so long as I kept 'my finger on the pulse' (or perhaps 'a toe in the water' would be a better simile) I had a profitable business. But a year or so later, a small incident was to show me that there still remained something missing in my life.

I had not really noticed the insignificant little shop attached to a house down in Douglas near the town centre. It had been there for some years selling knick-knacks of the kind that did not interest me, and if I had been asked, I would probably have had no knowledge of it at all. But suddenly it changed, and I saw it. Noticing the difference, I glanced in the window. Books had replaced the knick-knacks – but these were a different kind of book. These were religious. I read some of the titles. Thoughts of the stories my friend Alan had told after lights out at school came flooding back. One or two of the titles in the tiny window apparently told the stories of people whose lives had been changed by Jesus Christ. I remembered with a stab of conscience that I, too, had given my life to Jesus, but that it had not really done much for me. My conscience pricked because I knew it was my fault. I didn't see what could be done about it, but the books here looked interesting, and I thought a glance inside the shop would be a good idea.

I was a little self-conscious to find myself the only person apart from the assistant in the shop, but having walked in, I felt I couldn't simply walk out again, so I took a book from a shelf with my toes, sat down on the floor and flipped the pages. Soon I replaced that one and took another, quickly forgetting everything around me to become engrossed in the books.

'Hi,' said a man's voice next to me. I had not been aware of anyone else coming in the shop.

'Hi,' I responded, looking up briefly at the stranger, but I didn't know him, so quickly returned to the book. After a moment of silence, I returned the book to its place and reached up with my foot to the top shelf at my head height. I pulled another book out with my toes, sat on the floor again, and turned over the pages.

'You manage very well,' said the stranger in an accent very familiar to me.

'Yes,' I said, with a brief, non-committal smile. I was engrossed in the book, but noted the accent subconsciously.

'It's good to have a new Christian bookshop in Douglas, isn't it?' he continued, apparently wanting to talk.

'Yes,' I said again, although I didn't really take much notice of what he had said. My thoughts were whirling around. As I scanned the books here in this little shop, I remembered Alan and his Christian fervour; I remembered my own childish commitment to Christ and was now confronted with similar stories and commitment.

The stranger gave up trying to make conversation and after a while left the shop. When he had gone I frowned to myself. The man had obviously come from Northern Ireland. I should have paid more attention to him. Perhaps I had been rude. I went over to the assistant.

'Do you happen to know the man who was just here?' I asked.

'Yes,' the lady answered. 'He is Pastor David Gordon of Broadway Baptist Church. He hasn't been with us very long, but he is already making a big difference to our fellowship.' She grinned broadly, obviously a great fan of the pastor.

I gave her the money for a book, and saying 'goodbye' left the shop, but I could not forget that stranger. He was young and friendly, and not a bit like the stuffy ministers I had been used to from going to church at school. Not only that, he was obviously an Ulsterman. I could relate to a minister like that. I realised that I felt an instant affinity with him, even though I had not returned his conversation. I began to regret it. I should have spoken to him more – I hadn't been very polite.

I began to wonder what his church would be like. I reckoned it wouldn't be like the boring services I had had to put up with at school. The shop assistant seemed to have a good opinion of him. Perhaps I might venture to visit the church and see what it was like . . . The next Sunday I decided to risk it. I waited until the evening service, then jumped into my car and drove off to have a look.

The church itself was rather disappointing. I don't know what I expected it to look like, but it looked no different from any other imposing, ordinary church, as far as I could see. There were three blocks of pews separated by two aisles, and a large pulpit set high above the floor at the front. It looked dilapidated, damp and depressing. About a dozen people gathered together in the centre block. I placed myself in a pew on the left side away from the other people.

When Pastor Gordon began to speak, however, suddenly I noticed a difference. He did not climb the steps up into the pulpit as I had expected, but spoke from the floor, moving around and speaking directly to the congregation, face to face. This was definitely new. I had never seen a minister doing this before. He smiled, cracked a joke or two, but more particularly, spoke sincerely and enthusiastically. I liked his delivery. My affinity with him became stronger. I could learn from this man, I thought.

On the next Sunday, I went to the church for the morning service. There were a few more people this time, and those who had seen me the previous week welcomed me warmly. The pastor smiled broadly when he saw me come in, and I smiled back. I felt welcome and happy to be there.

From that time I went to church regularly with my Bible under my chin, and gradually got to know the members. They seemed very pleased to see me and welcomed me warmly each week. One of the most committed members was Kathy, who nearly always arrived at the church first. One morning, she welcomed me at the door as usual, but on this occasion she accompanied it with a friendly but rather over-enthusiastic thump on my back. My Bible, which had been in its usual place under my chin at the time, was sent flying across the floor, and in the momentum of the thump I lost my balance! Fortunately another friend, Avril, stood nearby and between them they just managed to save me from another fall on my face.

Kathy was mortified and apologised profusely, of course, but Avril pointed out to her that she really had to be more careful and temper her welcomes a little where Brian was concerned! However, it all went to make me feel more accepted and part of the fellowship, and we laughed about it for a long time afterwards. I remember Kathy fondly, for some time later she developed a kidney disease requiring a transplant which she did not survive, and she is now in the presence of her Lord. We will all never forget her enthusiasm for God's work and the commitment she gave to the work of his church here on earth.

Only one small problem bothered me a little in those early days at the church. At the start of the 'overhead projector'

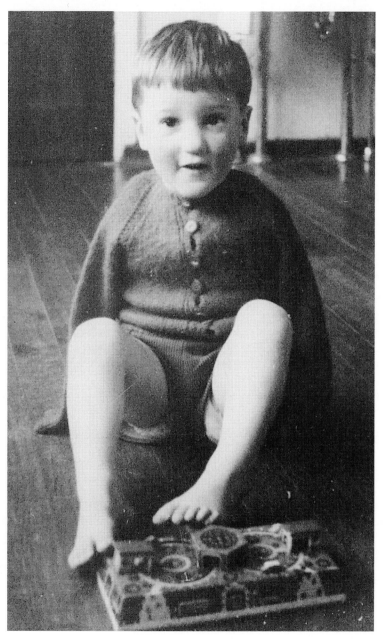

'It's my toy – hands off!' My first visit to the Princess
Margaret Rose Hospital, aged 2 years and 3 months

At the age of 4, getting a loving cuddle from Mum

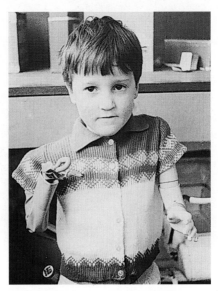

'Just leave me alone!'
As you can probably tell from the sombre expression,
I was not averse to the occasional tantrum

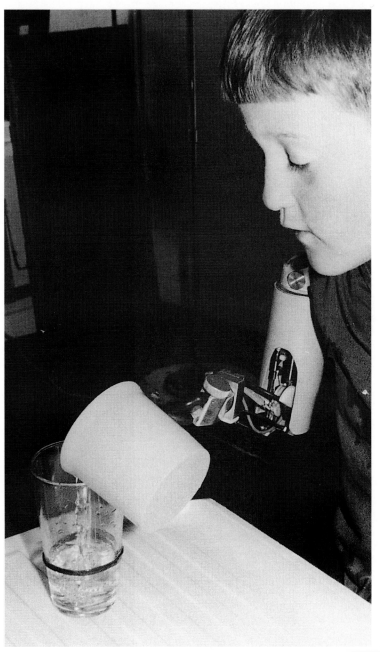

A trainee waiter – at the age of 7

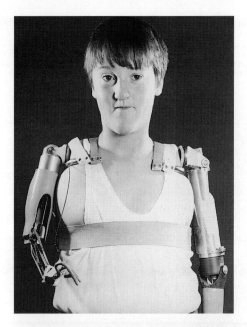

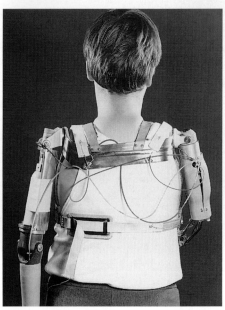

This is as good as it gets! The last set of 'Bionic Man' arms
I endured before freedom!

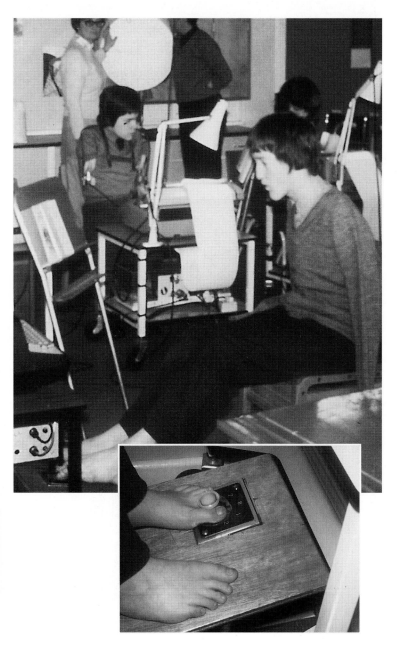

These toes were made for typing (see detail). That's me as a 14-year-old, hard at work at Fleming Fulton School, Belfast

I'm still typing today, but it's a little more high-tech now!

'Look, No Hands!' March 1999, at my home church in
Douglas, where I was commended to work in
partnership with 'Through the Roof'

A new beginning. Brian and May, 25 August 2000

revolution, many churches began to make use of the hundreds of new hymns and songs being written by doing away with their hymn-books or relegating them to a secondary position and using acetate sheets on a screen instead. Our church had not advanced to such 'new fangled machines' at the time, and still used the old hymn-books. I had two alternatives therefore, if I wished to join in the singing. Either, when everyone else stood, I would have to sit so that I could hold the hymn-book in my toes, or else I would need someone to hold the book for me. I did not like either method really, and my lack of self-confidence led me sometimes to sitting deliberately on my own just to see if anyone would think of me enough to come and sit with me! As my confidence grew, I got over the feelings of insecurity, but I must admit to being very glad when the overhead projector arrived and I could join in whole-heartedly without needing any help.

I soon found myself accepted as part of the group and began to be invited to their homes. I made many friends, particularly, as I anticipated, Pastor David Gordon, with whom I did indeed have an affinity. As I got to know him and his wife Heather better, I often enjoyed evenings with them and their children as we shared a meal together or simply laughed and relaxed. Often I would ask him to clarify some problem I had come up against or remembered from my childish faith, and before long, I realised that Jesus Christ was more real to me than ever before.

During those years when I had forgotten him and gone my own way, I had begun to doubt his existence and forget all I had been taught. Now he had brought me back to himself and I realised what I had been missing. A completely new life began for me; a life in obedience to God, but a life which was fulfilling and secure. I could look back and see that God had not abandoned me, but I had abandoned him. His hand had still remained on my life. He had led me to the little Bible bookshop where I met David Gordon who would, in turn, lead me back to a full relationship with God.

'In all things God works for the good of those who love him . . .' I remembered. I determined never to wander away again. My God would have my full commitment from now on. I could trust him completely with my life. I knew he would never let me down.

Now I had rediscovered God, I could never be 'half-hearted' again about following him. I could never give enough to repay the Saviour who gave everything to give me eternal life. Whatever I did from then on was going to count for God. If he was to have a free hand to direct my life then I, in turn, must give full and total commitment to whatever he put before me.

Now I had become a fully committed Christian, Pastor David discussed with me about taking the step of believers' baptism. He explained that in this touching and often emotional ceremony, one is immersed briefly in water to symbolise a personal repentance for sin and the grateful acceptance of God's forgiveness, together with the resolve to turn away from sin and begin a new life with God. Willing to obey God and do anything to consolidate my faith to myself and the world – although the thought of so public a ceremony terrified me – I agreed to be baptised, and looked forward to the opportunity of witnessing to everyone of my renewed faith.

However, as there were several others in a similar position, the pastor suggested that we should all meet together so that he could explain the implications of baptism more fully. This done and our final assent given, on Sunday 1 July 1984, in front of the evening congregation, I was baptised with five others.

First we each gave testimony as to how we came to a personal knowledge of Christ, and then one by one we stepped down into the baptismal pool. Normally, the pastor expected the candidate to hold on to his right hand with their left hand, while the pastor's left hand supported their head as they went backwards into the water. However, I presented something of a problem to Pastor David. He was not quite sure how to go about baptising someone with no hands with which to hang on! When my turn came, therefore, he clung on to my shirt, hoping the buttons would hold and that he wouldn't choke me to death or drown me! I responded to the vows of allegiance to God, then Pastor David slipped me beneath the water and up again. The joy that flooded through me cannot be described. I felt the presence of God almost tangibly, and knew that he would never leave me. I had announced to everyone in this symbolic way that my life belonged to God, and I would, with his help, prove it by obedience to him.

That summer, a team from Baptist Youth Evangelism arrived to work on the Isle of Man for outreaches lasting two weeks at a time over two years. This organisation arranged for dedicated young people gifted in evangelism to be seconded to help struggling churches for a set length of time. They might give a few weeks or so to BYE before going to university or college, as a way of giving some of their time to God, and go with ideas and enthusiasm to try to revitalise churches where invited. David Gordon had links with BYE from his former years in Northern Ireland, and he asked if a team could come and help his dwindling fellowship.

One of the first ideas they had for trying to meet and encourage young people into the church was to open a youth club in the basement of the church building. It had apparently been a club of some kind years before, for it sported dusty table tennis and snooker tables, above which were draped old fishing nets with glass ball weights and lobster pots dangling from them by way of decoration. The BYE team together with some of us from the church smartened everything up and reopened the club which we called the 'Salt Cellar'.

I, too, could see the possibilities for evangelism and pitched myself into it with a will. Helpers who only attended occasionally could be no good to the work. I made sure I went every week. I became a familiar sight climbing out of my car with my Bible tucked under my chin and things I needed for the evening in a bag held between my teeth.

Since I was a regular and enthusiastic member and committed leaders were needed, I was soon asked to become the treasurer. I took the task on gladly, collecting the fees from the young people and managing the general finances. It became a growing task. The club did, indeed, attract the young people of Douglas, and before long thirty to forty gathered in the basement for lively times of fun with a great deal of noise! Then, with my available transport, my tasks widened into collecting the 'tuck' for sale during the evenings.

When supplies were needed, I would take myself off to the wholesaler's with the Salt Cellar cheque book and the member-ship card to fill up the car with sweets, cans and crisps. An evening without 'tuck' was unthinkable to the lively crowd of young people, and the small profit made on sales helped towards the expenses of running the club. While they munched and gulped Coke they kept up games of table tennis, snooker, table football and darts accompanied by the obligatory loud music.

Sometimes in the summer we would go off to the beach to play uno-hockey in which I would invariably be the goalkeeper. The game would be fast and furious, often resulting in the stick heads snapping and flying off in the fierce clashes. Afterwards we often cooled down in the Ranch Café for a bacon bap or juice drink. It would come as something of a surprise to me to see the waitresses' bemused looks when they realised I had no arms and wondered how I was going to eat my bacon bap. Their eyes would nearly pop as they saw me swing my left leg over my right knee to pick up my snack with my toes! My friends were soon used to the way I handled everything, and hardly noticed the difference. In fact, they even became a little irritated by the amazement of strangers.

To my friends I simply did everything with toes instead of fingers – it was no big deal. To see the incredulity on the faces of strangers became boring and even intrusive to them. They forgot that in the beginning, they, too, could not avoid the looks of surprise and wonder!

The BYE team helped us with a great deal of outreach in the two years that followed. They had intended only to come to us for one summer, but apparently they enjoyed themselves so much that they wanted to return again the next year! In fact, just as my father had done earlier, one or two members of the team fell in love with the Isle of Man, and stayed on with us permanently. They are my good friends to this day.

The influence of the BYE team lingered on. Several of the young people from the youth club turned their lives over to Christ and joined the church fellowship. But Pastor David Gordon's step of inviting the team was not the only influence for good in the church. He had other ideas – radical ones. If people were to be attracted to the damp, old and forbidding building, there would be a great deal of work to be done.

How would the older members take to change? Problems there may have been, but the dwindling original membership never had cause to regret inviting this enthusiastic and godly man to help them. His charismatic personality and pertinent sermons revitalised the existing congregation who excitedly saw more and more new people coming into the church to meet their Saviour. But David Gordon had hardly started . . .

10

'Wired to the moon'

I had not long been attending the church when things started to happen. The crumbling building needed a great deal of work to make it habitable. With only a small number of church members, there could not be enough money to solve all the problems, so a programme of patching up started. The first task was to try to stem the waterfall pouring through the roof and down the walls every time it rained. No more than absolute necessities could be completed, but it gave us the incentive to remove the fungus and algae growing profusely in the damp.

Then David instigated a truly radical change. He discussed making a space by removing the choir pews. This would provide a platform for all kinds of activities. Had the traditionally oriented congregation any idea about what would happen in that space, they might not have accepted the change so passively – but as it was, they watched the changes with interest.

When sufficient patching up had been done, we could begin to tackle the painting and varnishing. I felt I could play a useful part at this stage. I enthusiastically pitched in to help, and my contribution was gladly received. I may have been new to the congregation, but I did not remain shyly in the background. Work needed doing and I determined to do what I could. As in my own flats, I could adequately cope with all painting work below a six-foot-high level, so I claimed all the skirting-boards, doors and lower walls. With a brush in my toes I set to work together with the rest of the team of workers. It was hard work, but we joyfully got on with it, and had much fun at the same time.

Of course, sometimes I had to lie on my back in order to reach my sections. It caused some concern to the ladies when they saw me stretched out on the cold floor in the foyer, varnishing the stairs and banisters.

'You'll catch a chill lying on the damp floor like that!' they scolded, but they were fascinated by the way I managed.

My life now took on another dimension. I had my work at the Harbour Board and the flats to administer, but now I had a church family too. My sphere of friendships widened dramatically, and my natural shyness declined. I soon felt secure in the group and free to be myself. I noticed that my new friends did not regard me as 'helplessly' disabled, but as unique in my own way, and gladly accepted me for myself.

Soon we began to see how useful the new space vacated by the pews was to be. The days of having only preachers and listeners in church had passed. Now many aspects of worship could be experienced and enjoyed by the worshippers. Instrumentalists needed room to lead the worship either together with or sometimes instead of the organ. Sometimes speakers preferred a more 'friendly' approach to their listeners rather than being removed 'six feet above contradiction', as one member quipped, into the high pulpit; others could testify face to face with the listeners as to what God meant to them. But perhaps the most radical aspect of new worship came in the form of drama and dance – much to the surprise and apprehension of the traditionalists. So many different kinds of worship described in the Bible had been forgotten for so long. Now many different gifts and talents given by God could be exercised in the worship.

With an improved church and meaningful services, soon new people began to join the small congregation, and this in turn encouraged others to attend. It was a good start, but David had even bigger ideas for the future.

His dream was to see the church full, and workers within it who could reach out to the surrounding population. Church was not a club for the few. David and those of us who had come to a knowledge of God wanted more than anything to spread the message of salvation – and our church should provide a base for God to work through us.

I thoroughly enjoyed all my involvement with church activities. It provided me not only with a very active social life, but gave me opportunities to talk about the Lord Jesus Christ. The youth club became a central part of my life in particular, and every Saturday night we arranged some special event when we could have fun. Activities included Bible studies, games, treasure hunts and walks, and most of them included food! Being the only one with transport of my own, I eventually found myself ferrying carloads of teenagers from place to place – and I have to admit to a measure of showing off while I did it!

'Look at his feet spinning that steering wheel!' one would say. 'It seems so fast!'

As they watched, I would mischievously take one foot off the accelerator to fiddle with the radio. Wondering glances told me how impressed they all were. Once, the radiator gave me some trouble, which meant that my windscreen kept steaming up –

especially with a car-load of friends, all talking and laughing. Knowing how puzzled they would be, I kept lifting one foot and wiping the windscreen.

'What on earth are you doing?' shouted someone. 'How can you drive if your foot is up there?'

'Be careful!' shouted another, terrified.

'Don't worry,' I laughed. 'You're quite safe!' But I don't think they were convinced.

One Saturday evening as usual my Mini was crammed with young people whom I was delivering to their homes after the meeting. The wide, main road past the grandstand where the TT races commence gave me ample opportunity to show how well I could drive and as it was quite late, there was not much traffic about. I manoeuvred the steering wheel and controls with my toes, knowing that my friends were fascinated by my perform-ance. Then, among the general noise and jocularity, a voice raised itself above the rest.

'There's a police car behind us!' shouted Sara.

I glanced in my mirror, but I could see no blue lights. 'Oh, yes?' I said, grinning. I was not going to fall for that one. I forged ahead.

'There is!' someone else called. I looked again, but could see nothing.

'Sure!' I replied, leaning on the accelerator.

Only when I reached the next traffic lights did I discover that they had not been kidding. The police Land Rover had been so much taller than my small Mini that the blue light could not be seen through my rear window. The officer asked me to get out of the car.

'Sir, do you know what speed you were doing just now?' he asked with a frown.

'I'm very sorry,' I murmured, 'I'm afraid not — perhaps my

speedometer is broken . . .' Giggles and bursts of laughter came from within the car.

'Do you know what the speed limit is on that piece of road you've just been driving along?'

'Er . . . Yes, officer. It's thirty miles per hour,' I stammered, embarrassed.

'Well,' said the officer sternly, 'I had to do considerably more than that just to keep up with you.'

'I really am sorry,' I grovelled. I had been taking no notice of my speed at all.

'Well,' continued the policeman, 'I will simply caution you this time, but make sure it doesn't happen again.'

My face red, I got back gratefully into the car, and drove off very carefully indeed, but I was never allowed to forget the rebuke. From that time on, my friends nicknamed me 'Speedy Gonzales' (from the popular song), and I can't say that I made any real effort to change until I grew somewhat older and wiser!

I had been attending the church for about three years when the year of 1987 proved unforgettable for three very different reasons. The first was a disaster; the second, a once-in-a-lifetime thrill; and the third, another complete change in my life.

The disaster began right in at the New Year on Wednesday 14 January, during a thaw at the end of a bitterly cold spell of weather. A light sprinkling of snow still lay on the ground on what had been a very ordinary day. I had battled with my ledgers and bookkeeping at the Harbour Board, and looked forward to the usual home group Bible study at 8.00 p.m. in the home of one of the members. The study was well under way when the phone rang. Surprisingly, it was for me. My dad sounded worried.

'You'd better get round to Hutchinson Square right away,' he said, anxiously. 'I've had a telephone call from the fire service . . . something's wrong.'

I did not linger to ask questions, but as I drove round to the Square my mind spun into overdrive as I feared the worst. Was the place on fire? Had someone been hurt – or, perish the thought – even killed?

I could hear a fire alarm blaring out from the flats as I approached, and my heart leaped when I saw the fire engine blocking the way, forcing me to park some distance away. I jumped out of the car and sprinted the rest of the way. I looked for the smoke but could see none, so I assumed, thankfully, that the place was not on fire. A fire officer directed me into the building that was in total darkness other than the emergency lighting system in the hall, but as soon as I stepped through the door I could hear the trouble. Water was cascading down the main staircase, flooding the ground floor to a depth of about thirty centimetres – and it was rising!

'We can't find the stop-tap, Mr Gault,' shouted the fire officer above the din of rushing water. 'Do you know where it is?'

I had done my homework well when I bought the flats. Not much remained that I did not know about them. I quickly ran to show the fire officer where he could turn off the devastating flow. Then we searched for the root of the problem.

It did not take long to discover that the cold-water storage tank in the attic space had frozen, and with the thaw the main pipe had cracked severely. Hundreds and hundreds of gallons of water had poured down through the four floors. The residents had been drenched as they obeyed the insistent call of the fire alarms to evacuate the building, but we were all grateful for the fact that the water had poured straight down the stairwell, and so bypassed four of the six flats. The two on the ground floor had born the brunt of the onslaught.

As I stared at the devastation, I thanked God that the situation had not been worse and asked for calmness of heart and mind as

I arranged to clear up the mess in the days that lay ahead. My first priority had to be to find alternative accommodation for the tenants in the two worst affected flats. The second priority was to have a plumber drain the cold-water tank in the attic, shut it off, and find an alternative and much safer means of supplying the only flat that relied on its supply. I needed peace of mind that this would never happen again! I was relieved to find that I had the full co-operation of the insurance company, and their assessor proved to be very helpful, so I could get on with the repairs immediately.

I had no idea that water could cause so much damage. Over the following six weeks, kind friends helped me to get the flats back to shape. We moved damaged furniture and hauled sodden, ruined carpets out into skips. Then an electrician loosened all the light fittings and switches so they would have an opportunity to dry out properly in the warmth of industrial heaters which I hired to draw the water from walls and floorboards. For several weeks it felt like a tropical greenhouse when you entered through the front door!

Six weeks later, on 27 February, the painter and decorators had completed their work, new carpets had been fitted, and all the flats were fully occupied once more. I had done all I could to make sure nothing similar ever happened again.

The second event proved just as much of a surprise, but this time a very pleasant one. Cath and Eric Quirk had taken me 'under their wing' when I started to attend the church. They were a tower of strength to me spiritually, and I have good reason to thank them for their loving support. One day Cath rang me.

'Could you pop round and see us very soon?' she said. 'We have something to discuss with you.'

I agreed, but wondered what was so important or mysterious that she couldn't give me some idea about it over the phone. As usual, Cath welcomed me into her home with her warm, radiant smile. I must have still looked puzzled as we sat down.

'It's like this,' she began. 'David has been approached by the BBC as to whether our church can provide some input when *Songs of Praise* comes to the Isle of Man this year.' She paused and the grin spread across her face again. 'I suggested to him that you would be a possible candidate to give testimony on the programme, so we have nominated you.'

I could not have been more flabbergasted! 'But I can't do that!' I protested as all my inherent shyness came rushing back. 'What could I say?'

Cath tried to reassure me. 'You just answer the questions you are asked, but tell them how you feel about the Lord Jesus Christ,' she said. 'You'll love it! Although, of course,' she added quickly, 'the decision as to whether you are chosen is not ours. I suppose the producers decide whom they will have from the nominations.'

I understood that, but as I said 'goodbye' to Cath and Eric, my mind was in turmoil. I had to do some serious thinking. This was not just a simple matter as to whether or not I wanted to appear on television – even if I happened to be chosen. Other issues had to be resolved if I was to declare my faith so publicly.

As I drove home, I mulled over the position. As always, I could not do anything half-heartedly. If I gave testimony on television, it would be all or nothing. I would explain that God took first place in my life – above everything. And if this was true, then I had to come to terms with a matter that had been bothering me for about eighteen months.

During this time, David's sermons and my own Bible reading had drawn me increasingly to two passages in Isaiah, which spoke vividly of the strength to be received from the Lord while ministering to the poor and needy: 'if you spend yourselves on behalf of the hungry and satisfy the needs of the oppressed, then your light will rise in the darkness . . . The Lord will guide you always,' the prophet Isaiah stated (Isaiah 58:10–11). 'Those who hope in the Lord will renew their strength. They will soar on wings like eagles; they will run and not grow weary, they will walk and not be faint.'

What was the Lord saying to me in particular about these verses? I read them over and over. I knew God was speaking to me, but what did he want me to do? I thought rationally. I had come to know the one true God who took the punishment for and forgave my sin. I therefore wanted everyone to know about it and that their sins could be forgiven too.

My life now belonged to God and I wanted to obey him in everything. What did he want me to do with my life, then? Was there some better way I could serve him and tell others about him? Bible college sprang to mind.

I discussed my questions with a few of my closest friends and with David himself. I knew that David had gone to Bible college in order to learn more about God so that he could minister more effectively. Perhaps I could do with this kind of training in order to carry out God's instructions to help the poor and needy. But I had a very good job with the Harbour Board. If I went to Bible college it would mean giving up that job, and after the disappointments of finding a job in the first place, I dreaded having to begin all over again if Bible college should prove a mistake.

And what on earth would my parents say? They were sympathetic to my church activities, but I doubted whether they would be so sympathetic if I told them I intended to give up my excellent job to go off to Bible college. And where would it get me? What prospects would I have when I had finished the course? I may have had an adequate living coming from the flats, but I needed fulfilment too. What would Bible college equip me to do?

As my thoughts turned over and over, I realised that I would have to settle the problem once and for all if I should be asked to declare my faith on television. Half measures would not do. I had to be fully committed to the will of God or there could be nothing to say to others. It also meant that I would have to discuss it with my parents. I knew what they would say: 'You must be wired to the moon!' The old Irish expression rang through my thoughts. Was I indeed crazy to think of giving up a secure future with the Harbour Board for the uncertain future of Bible college and beyond?

There could only be one answer, of course. I had to do God's will first. If he called me to go to Bible college, then he would open the doors for me. The way to find out would be to apply to a college and see what happened. If I should be offered a place, then I would take it from the Lord that I must accept it. Soon afterwards, I heard that a place had been reserved for me on a year's course at Capernwray Bible School in Lancashire, England.

With a place offered to me, suddenly my mind filled with doubts. If I accepted the place, there would be many difficulties to overcome. It was one thing to be offered a place, but who would help me when I needed help? Would I be able to manage the written work? After all, I had fallen back in my work at business college – I could just not write fast enough with my toes. I did not want to fail with another course. Then there were the more practical details: Who would wash my hair? And worst of all to my mind: who would tuck in my shirt? I hated not being able to do this simple task. I may have acquired a great deal of flexibility throughout my life, but it was just not possible for me to manipulate my legs and feet enough to tuck a shirt into my trousers. Suppose the college was so warm that I could not wear a jumper to disguise the problem? Perhaps I was being a fool to leave my good job to go to Bible college anyway.

'Don't worry,' Cath and Eric assured me again and again. 'You're worrying unnecessarily. You'll be fine. It doesn't matter about your shirt a bit. No one will even notice.'

For the umpteenth time I knocked on their door for reassurance.

'I must be sure it's the right thing,' I fretted. 'I couldn't face Mum and Dad if I made a mess of things.'

Cath smiled. 'Have you prayed about it and asked God to direct you?' she said.

'Of course,' I replied.

'Well, *has* he directed you? Have you found any leading through your Bible reading?'

'Well, yes,' I falteringly admitted.

'Do you feel that God has opened doors for you?' Cath persisted.

'I've been accepted for Capernwray,' I said, brightening.

'Have you had any leading other than Bible college?'

'No, I suppose not,' I had to agree.

'Well, then,' Cath rested her case. 'What more do you want?'

I grinned. Did I trust God or not? How else did I expect him to show me the way forward, and if he led me, then he would surely take care of the details – even the problem of tucking in my shirt!

I wrote accepting the place and looked forward to commencing the course in September the following year. But *Songs of Praise* would happen before that time came, and I soon learned that I had indeed been accepted for interview on the programme. I began to get my thoughts in order.

First I had to tell my parents and the rest of the family of my decision to go to Bible college. I had put the day off too long even now, so I took a deep breath and told them. Their reaction was much as I had expected. They listened carefully, but they did not really understand my motives. They were naturally apprehensive about me giving up my hard-won job for an uncertain future, but they had enough confidence in me to know that I would not have started down this path without a great deal of thought. I explained that I felt God was leading me in this direction and that I trusted him to take care of my future, and that I was sure he had some work for me to do for him.

They listened and tried to understand, but I knew that I could only make them see how God leads through my experience. They would discover how God cares for and leads his people as they watched my obedience to God's command – and then they would understand. I did not fully understand myself, of course, but I would trust God and obey.

11

Songs of Praise

The first week of June is always the busiest time on the Isle of Man because this is when 45,000 motorcyclists descend upon it for the TT races. Mayhem reigns as normal services are disrupted, every guest-house and hotel is full to capacity (including that of my parents, of course), and the noise of thundering bikes can be heard reverberating across the Island. There is not much choice for the Island residents but to accept the phenomenon and 'go with the flow', leaving any important business to other weeks.

The filming of *Songs of Praise*, therefore, was wisely set for the second week of June after most of the motorcyclists and the crowds had gone home. For those of us who were to be involved with the programme, however, the fun was just beginning!

Songs of Praise is a popular, long-running series which aims to bring all kinds of Christians with their gifts, joys and sadnesses to the viewers. It is based at a different church each week, going around the country – and even the world – from place to widely differing place. During each programme, several individuals are interviewed and tell how their Christianity or view of God has affected their lives. Then they each choose a hymn to be sung by the invited congregation in the church, while for the viewers, the words appear on their television screens so that they, too, can join in the singing.

The church chosen to feature in the filming here on the Isle of Man was St George's in the heart of Douglas, the capital town. Here the large invited congregation would be well accommodated together with the cameras, vast amount of equipment and the production team.

For weeks I had been looking forward to the excitement of the filming, plus the thrill of being interviewed by Roger Royle the presenter. Now excitement gave way to nerves as I frantically tried to form the words of what I would say. I turned for inspiration to one of David's sermons. I had heard and digested plenty, and chose one with three points all beginning with the letter 'T': Thanking God, Talking of God and Trusting God. This I concluded would be short, sharp and to the point for the anonymous listeners, and would get the message across. It would need to be short, sharp and to the point, for I had been allocated just three minutes for my interview!

I mulled over the points of the sermon in my mind for days, trying to condense all David said into three minutes flat. I practised time and time again, but found that my version lost something in the condensation! I practised harder and more frantically, determining to make sure I managed to get a good message over in that short time. But as the day of filming drew near, I had still not achieved my aim. Lying on my bed in my room, I decided not to go downstairs for a cup of coffee as was my custom, but to go for a walk in the warm summer evening air to see if I could sort things out in my mind. Slipping into my shoes that I had left in their usual place at the bottom of the stairs, I went out to the car.

I decided to go up to Marine Drive just beyond Douglas Head, and then park and walk along the coast. I could go no further in the car anyway, because part of the road had collapsed some years before, but although motor vehicles were prohibited from going on, it was considered safe for walkers. By the time I arrived it was about 8.45 p.m., and it had begun to get cooler as the sun disappeared. Seeing a couple sitting in their car looking out at the view, I knocked on the window with my toes.

'Would you mind buttoning my jacket for me?' I asked. 'I am going for a long walk and it's getting rather chilly.'

The couple looked surprised, but one of them did as I asked and I trotted away towards the headland. I walked for about an hour, and then as it had got rather dark by then, I made my way back to the car, drove home, and went to bed – still without any firm idea of what I would say on the programme.

At about 10.30 p.m. the front doorbell rang. My dad answered it and found two policemen standing on the doorstep.

'We've had a report that a man with no arms asked a couple in a car to fasten his jacket, and then disappeared around the headland,' one of them said, seriously. 'We've been to look, but can find no vehicle or person answering the description in the area. Since there are not many folk on this island without arms, we wondered if you could tell us anything about this.'

Dad was completely baffled because as far as he knew I had called 'goodnight' some time earlier and gone up to my room. My shoes were once again at the foot of the stairs, so he knew I must be in. He did not know that I had been out for an hour or so earlier! He shouted up to me, and I came down to see what was going on.

'Ah,' said the policeman with a grin when I explained where I had been. 'Well, sir,' he went on. 'You see, that part of the coast is unfortunately notorious for suicides, and the couple in the car whom you asked to button your jacket were afraid that you might be thinking of the same thing. They thought they had better let us know about it!'

I apologised for the trouble I had caused, and promised to let someone know if I intended to go off for a lone walk again!

Harold Moore, my boss at the Harbour Board, was delighted when the BBC researcher asked him if he would allow me to be filmed and interviewed in my office. He agreed enthusiastically, and I made a special attempt to tidy it up for the filming.

I always tidied up before the weekend, leaving my current work strewn about the floor for the rest of the week. It may have looked untidy, but I left my papers exactly where I wanted them – just as people with arms would leave their work on a desk. But since the filming took place on a weekday, my usual tidying session had to be put forward for once.

On the day of the interview, I could not subdue a feeling of nervous anticipation. It is not every day that someone like me gets to be filmed for television, and I felt the full responsibility of the occasion. What if I made a mess of the whole thing? I would not only let down David and my friends who had nominated me, but the entire watching public. I had a responsibility to tell them about Jesus Christ. I *must* get it right!

Roger Royle and the team were very welcoming and kind when they finally arrived and we were introduced. I have to admit to being somewhat overawed at meeting such a famous personality, but he quickly put me at my ease and we talked freely. I was soon to discover that my three-minute interview would take three hours of filming!

Eventually it all began, but to start with they decided to film me driving my car along Douglas Promenade to demonstrate how I coped with it. A cameraman and technician complete with equipment crammed into the rear seat of my latest car, a

Ford Escort, while I drove off along the seafront. To add to the interior shots, we were also accompanied by a van driving parallel to get exterior 'long shots'. Inside the car with me, the camera-man pointed the camera at my feet where I turned the steering wheel with my toes and manipulated the other controls. I proudly put my foot down on the accelerator – as usual – only to notice frantic gesticulations from the van. 'Slow down! Slow down!' they were clearly indicating!

The interview in my office came next, with me sitting by the window and backed by the beautiful view across Douglas Bay with the 'Tower of Refuge' on the horizon. The cameras whirred and I began my three-point sermon. Before many seconds had passed I had got myself into a corner and had to stop.

Roger Royle smiled kindly. 'Don't worry,' he said, 'we'll have another try, but be yourself.'

I tried again. First 'Thanking God'. I had a lot to thank him for, but it took too long to say so.

'Cut,' called the producer.

Roger Royle smiled again. 'Look,' he said, 'don't try to preach to the people – there just isn't time for that. Be yourself, tell them about your gifts and the message will speak for itself.'

I realised I would have to forget David's excellent sermon and take another tack altogether. It was suggested that I sit on the floor and show how I got my work done. The cameras rolled again. I picked up my pen in my toes and wrote on a piece of paper. Then, I demonstrated how I used a ruler and a calculator, picking out the numbers carefully with my agile big toe.

'So the gift that God gives to others with their fingers . . .' said Roger Royle.

'That's right,' I responded, 'God has provided me with my toes.'

'But you are about to give yourself even more difficulties, aren't you – because you are soon leaving the Island and moving to the mainland. What are you going to be doing there?' Roger steered me towards explaining my faith.

'Yes, I'm going to college – Bible college,' I told him. 'I see that as being obedient to God. Over the past eighteen months the Lord has been opening doors for me and saying, "Brian, I want more from you! I want you to be obedient and go out and share the joy and hope that you have with others, and be an encourager to others." '

'But this is a huge risk, Brian,' said Roger Royle. 'You know the people here. You know the people you work with, and you have your church and your family here.'

'I will always still have them,' I said eagerly. 'They will be praying for me, and by the strength they give me through their prayers, I'll be able to go out and serve the Lord in whatever capacity he wants me to take in the days ahead.'

'So what hymn have you chosen?' asked Roger, indicating that the interview had run its time.

'I've chosen "Meekness and majesty" by Graham Kendrick,' I told him.

'Why?' asked Roger, simply.

'Because it's a worship song to King Jesus!' I exclaimed enthusiastically. I could choose no other hymn because this one always stood out in my mind as a powerful example of the description of Jesus's suffering for us. The words seem to 'blow my mind' and bring a lump to my throat. It describes the wonder and amazement that Jesus – wholly man and wholly God – suffered such an awful death on a cross to give me, Brian Gault, forgiveness, acceptance, peace, love and *life*! I wonder anew each time that I get to the last few lines:

Lord of infinity, stooping so tenderly,
Lifts our humanity to the heights of his throne.

In all our struggles, weaknesses, tears, laughter and joys, Jesus is our hope and our assurance both now and in the future! What a concept!

The three hours of filming with its three-minute interview soon ended, and I was left to worry whether I had got my points over or not. I had only one chance. Had I 'blown' it? Did the Lord Jesus come across as supreme? Or had Brian taken the stage?

Mum and Dad soon informed me. I have to confess that the short time on *Songs of Praise* spoke more to my family than all the thousands of words I ever shared in their presence. I may still be 'wired to the moon' in their understanding of my faith, but now there was a real acceptance of my heading off for Bible college.

Mum told me that the phone did not stop ringing for many days after the programme went out on Sunday 15 November 1987. There was great excitement as friends, family and acquaintances all rang to say how much they had enjoyed seeing me and hearing what I had to say. But the greatest thrill came when the Chief (Prime) Minister of the Isle of Man, Miles Walker, telephoned to express his appreciation of my part of the programme. Mum and Dad were overwhelmed with pride. Their Brian had appeared on television and had received a response from the Chief Minister himself! It was a wonderful accolade!

That, however, was not the finish of it all. For the next few weeks, we received a response from the general public from all over the British Isles. Letters, cards and poems – particularly from the disabled – poured in to encourage me to keep going in my studies, and to assure me of their love and prayers! It was quite wonderful! So many people had watched the programme and felt an affinity with me – enough to respond by writing. I felt humbled and very grateful to them, but even more grateful to God for all he had done for me and for my mum and dad through this short programme.

I have kept one of the poems sent to me by a lady in Scotland who was confined to a wheelchair. Its author is unknown, but it touched me deeply and I remember it every time I feel like giving up:

I asked God for strength, that I might achieve –
I was made weak, that I might learn humbly to obey.
I asked for health, that I might do greater things –
I was given infirmity, that I might do better things.
I asked for riches, that I might be happy –
I was given poverty, that I might be wise.
I asked for power, that I might have the praise of men –
I was given weakness, that I might feel the need of God.
I asked for all things, that I might enjoy life –
I was given life that I might enjoy all things.
I got nothing that I asked for –
But everything I had hoped for.
Almost despite myself, my unspoken prayers were answered.
I am among all men most richly blessed.

12

A student again

I arrived at Capernwray Hall, near Camforth in Lancashire, to discover I was one of nearly two hundred students from twenty-three different countries of the world. A large proportion were American or Canadian, but it amazed me that so many national-ities were represented, with all their different backgrounds and cultures. The male dormitories were housed in what had once been the stable block in the hall's heyday, and although privacy was at a premium, we soon settled in and got to know each other.

Ian, who had once served in the Household Cavalry, occupied the bed next to mine, and frequently scared me half to death in the middle of the night when in his sleep he suddenly yelled 'Shut up!' or 'Atten . . . *tion*!' He became a good friend, however, and solved a few of my problems by agreeing to wash my hair for me, and to tuck in my shirt.

Part of the college ethos included all students helping with 'work duties' in addition to the course work. These ranged from work on the college farm to the general maintenance of buildings and grounds and domestic duties. Since I possessed administrative skills, I was allocated to the college office on Friday mornings, where I assisted with the day-to-day ledger accounts. Some might well have considered this less than enjoyable, but I found it a therapeutic change from the previous four days of lectures and personal study, and tackled the job with a will.

Friday nights were set aside for fun at the Friday Night Live session when we would all sit around the log fire in the lounge and relax. The programme consisted of personal testimonies, songs and drama, among many other things. Together with the healthy cultural rivalries between the nationalities, it all went to make lively evenings that often left our face muscles weak with laughter!

Sometimes during these evenings we shared with each other where we felt the Lord might be calling us to serve him. Among the students were a group of tall, blond-haired beauties from Norway. It was quite uncanny how many of the fellows began to feel a call to serve in Norway!

Ron Tambatamba, a student from Zambia, impressed me greatly. He was a married man with five children who simply overflowed with thankfulness and joy at being able to learn more and share his love for Jesus. Even when all his luggage became lost at Heathrow Airport, leaving him with only the clothes he stood up in, his face never lost its smile and his heart retained a firm trust in God. The other students responded in the only way possible – by giving him new shirts, ties, trousers and many other accessories he needed. It was wonderful to see the radiance and spontaneity of thankfulness flowing from Ron's heart to God!

But there were times when Ron's face lost its smile. I often saw tears flowing down his face at the wastage of food after college meals. As he saw the bins filling up with leftover food, he would remember the many times at home in Zambia when God had provided food and basic necessities for his wife and children when otherwise they would have starved. It was a sobering thought to those of us who had always had plenty to eat.

Our days soon got into a pattern of lectures, study and recreation, but we all looked forward to the highlight of the week – the stampede after the first morning lecture to collect the post! With most of us many miles from our homes and families, we awaited the arrival of letters eagerly.

What an encouragement a few words from friends or relations were to us! No matter what the insignificant message might be, it all added up to 'We are thinking of you', and that was what mattered. However, a couple of months after the term began, I found myself envied more than the rest because my 'G' pigeon-hole was crammed with letters in response to the *Songs of Praise* programme which had gone out in November! It was great to read them all, but I soon came down to earth as the deluge gradually trickled to a halt and my 'moment of fame' declined.

I found myself in demand once more for an entirely different purpose when the college laundry room was reduced to one tumble-drier. With nearly two hundred students trying to get clothes dry in the damp winter atmosphere, my car and I became the only access to the launderette in nearby Carnforth! My Ford Escort soon knew the way almost on its own – until the college driers were once more restored to full working order.

Most weeks throughout the course we were required to complete written assignments of between six hundred and a thousand words. From the start this prospect had caused me most nervousness because I had no idea whether I would be able to write fast enough to keep up. In the first place the lecturers spoke so quickly that I could not make comprehensive notes. I realised, therefore, that if I couldn't manage this much, then there would not be much hope for the assignments. However, the college thoughtfully always arranged for the students to be allocated to a 'family group' of about twelve members who were expected to help one another. A member of my group, Linda, had been a schoolteacher, and she nobly helped whenever my notes failed me. I shall always be grateful to her for giving up her valuable time to assist me. Without her help I might not have managed to complete the course adequately.

After our essays had been assessed and returned, each Tuesday night at 8 p.m., a different member of the group had to lead a Bible study based on the essay we had all written the previous week. I found these very precious evenings, less so with regard to the study – although it was always good – but more for the worship, sharing, caring and praying for one another. Each member of the group came from such a diversity of cultures, experiences and churches throughout the world, and yet all longed to become the kind of men and women God desired them to be.

The in-depth study and closeness to God made a great impression on us all, and I felt closer to him than ever before. So close, in fact, that I had not been at Capernwray for more than two months when I began to sense the direction in which God required me to move next.

I suppose the more studying we did, the more I, in particular, realised how much there still remained to learn, and I began to think about taking further specialised and intensive training when my present course had finished. Moorlands Bible College in Dorset seemed to stand out in my thoughts, and after prayer and meditation, I became convinced that this was where God wanted me to go next. However, I had several months to complete at Capernwray first, so I lodged the thought in the back of my mind for the time being, determining to bring it again to the Lord when the time was right.

We were expected to undertake various outside activities throughout the course that would help us to decide where our giftings lay, plus giving us the opportunity to deal with a variety of people and situations. One of these took place for ten days during February, when small groups of students were involved in a hands-on exercise of putting our faith into practice within churches throughout Britain. With Sharon from Scotland, Nigel from England and Fiona from the USA, I headed off to a small village near Bridgewater in Shropshire. It was intended that we should be accommodated by members of the congregation, but in so small a church, rooms could be found only for the two girls. The result was that Nigel and I had to make do with the only accommodation that could be found for us – a caravan normally used by summer visitors.

Nigel's bed was at one end of the van and mine at the other, but still, in the below zero temperatures, I could hear his teeth chattering! Every few hours I would wake from a fitful sleep to rub my toes together in a vain attempt to generate some warmth. But during the day we both soaked up as much sympathy as we could from the village folk who compensated us with lavish hot food and warmth in their homes! As we went from door to door in our scheduled visitation work, we found that the word had got around about the two crazy students living in an unheated caravan in the depths of winter so that they could share the love of God! Personally, I believe the inclement conditions we endured gave us all more openings and opportunities to share our love for Jesus than anything else! God had turned a seemingly adverse situation into something he could use through our weakness.

During the spring of 1988, I joined a small team of five students to undertake a week-long programme of activities at

Cartmel Primary School. The little country school was set in an idyllic village famous for its horse racing and its priory, and at the time was fighting for its survival. We were assigned to provide a programme of lessons and activities to communicate our faith, and through which we ourselves would gain experience in dealing with children.

I had no trouble in gaining the attention of the little children. They watched in wonder as I played table tennis against the headteacher during an assembly. Their eyes opened wide in amazement as I held the bat under my chin and sent the ball flying over the net. Then they could hardly believe it as I showed them how I could hold a cup of lemonade in my toes and drain the last drop. My next trick was to open a yummy Twix bar with my toes, and to show how I could also reach to get a toothbrush to my mouth. The scrubbing noise reduced them all to laughter! I turned pages of a book, wrote with a pen in my toes and showed the hiding-place in my shoe for money and car keys. All this was greeted with the utmost delight and astonishment, and made it easier for me to explain how God in his love had compensated me for the lack of arms.

Later during the spring term we visited a hospice on Sunday mornings for nine weeks. Run by nuns, the hospice was situated near Lancaster and about eight miles from the college. Of all the assignments we were given during the year's course, I found this the most difficult. Here were terminally ill people from all kinds of background, colour, creed and age, and yet we found ourselves unsure of our purpose and role and seemed entirely inadequate to help them.

'Be natural,' urged the wise sister-in-charge. 'Be simply as God has transformed you in Christ. Be listeners, supportive and honest.'

We went nervously into the wards, but as I reached out my

foot to shake someone's hand, the barriers came tumbling down! The dear people temporarily forgot their sad state to be astonished at how I coped without arms, and often relaxed into revealing their fears, doubts and anxieties.

I am so thankful for the opportunities of being allowed to read small portions of Scripture to them, and to hold their hands between my toes, praying about their situation. Later, as I took a quiet stroll in the college grounds, my heart would be heavy with tears for the sadnesses I had seen and the helplessness I felt. Oh, how we had to depend on the Lord Jesus Christ at each visit! And how we admired the ministry of the selfless nuns with their fully committed servant hearts.

Throughout my life I have often found that good, long walks in the countryside helped to relax and revitalise my weary or downcast spirit. At Capernwray, being surrounded by many beautiful walks we were spoilt for choice, so that often on Sunday afternoons, the Ford Escort would be crammed with students and we would head off into the hills and lakes. Sitting on a rock looking across the valleys to the hills beyond always proved a good antidote to the spiritual indigestion we suffered after twenty-two hours of lectures during the week. We had so much to ponder upon; it reminded me of cows who chew the cud through several stomachs – chewing over and over again!

As I studied, learned and looked back over my life, I began to see a more complete picture. I observed how one's family and background provide the training for God's programme of future ministry. All the experiences of my childhood – the frustrations and the accomplishments – can be taken by God and used. I needed to throw off the wrong attitudes I had acquired: the fact that I doubted whether I could be useful to God and the wrong thinking that unless perfect I would not be acceptable. Gradually I came to understand that I am what God has made me, and what still remains to be changed, God is committed to completing!

At last I could thank God for creating me the way I am. I became convinced that I am not a biological accident with a meaningless existence, but that in his wisdom, God loved me and planned that I should exist. He gave me a life that is both responsible and meaningful, and has plans for me that are utterly good. I thanked him for the richness of life I enjoy, and asked him to forgive my doubts. I wondered and praised that although God is so great and I am so insignificant among his creatures, he has endowed me with worth and value in his kingdom.

In reflection, my time at Capernwray became invaluable inasmuch as it prepared me with a good and firm foundation in teaching, studying, interaction with the community, laughter and tears in the friendships made, plus special times to enjoy God. As I returned home to the Isle of Man, I sensed that God had begun my spiritual training in earnest, but that I still had a long way to go.

13

More study

The year's course of study at Capernwray finished in July 1988. In September I began a three-year course at Moorlands Bible College. With just a little help I had managed to keep up with all the written work at Capernwray, and although I anticipated that the essays might be a bit longer and perhaps more taxing at Moorlands, I expected to cope. Imagine how I felt when I discovered that the essays needed to be between 2,500 and 3,000 words! I would have to get down to some serious work – and for that I needed floor space. I immediately set myself to find a place where I could spread myself out – a place where I need not be disturbed and where all my books and papers would not have to be continually tidied up. I came across a suitable place up in the top level of the library and soon claimed it as my own for the coming six months.

Now much determination and a certain amount of personal pride came into play as I attempted to meet all my essay deadlines. Every evening until at least 11 p.m. I took up residence in the library where I would be plied with large mugs of coffee by special friends to keep me going. Occasionally when one of my friends thought I had been working too long and too hard, he would insist that I have a break and relax for a while. Without these promptings I would probably have worked all night sometimes!

Since the library became 'my' domain, one of the daily duties assigned to me was to replace all the books that had been borrowed on to their appointed shelves. I could carry five or six books – depending on their thickness – under my chin and balanced on my right shoulder. Then I would pick my way carefully up the spiral staircase to where most of the books were kept and, balancing with one leg on a chair, after a little practice I could manoeuvre the book in between several others on the shelf. It was rather harder on the higher shelves six feet up, but I would not let it overcome me. I kept this job for the entire three years of the course and surprisingly, I suppose, I only dropped my load a couple of times!

At least once each week I could not resist the lure of a drive with a crowd of others down to Boscombe, eight miles away near Bournemouth, where we tucked into yummy, hot, spicy kebabs. After our snack, we would walk along the shore where I loved to feel the sand in my toes and paddle in the sea – even if it was a freezing winter's night!

My anxieties about coming to college had always included the problem of washing my hair and getting my shirt tucked in. I did not need to worry at Moorlands because along my corridor there were plenty of very helpful lads who saw it as their duty to help me as and when necessary. Ironing was another matter, but I soon acquired a group of wonderful girls who took the job on a rota basis! I became the envy of every other lad in the college as the girls pampered and spoiled me!

When half-term holidays came round, I knew I would not be

able to get back to the Isle of Man for so short a break. I needed accommodation, just as I had when I had been at boarding-school. On one of these occasions, I visited a very dear couple who had seen me on *Songs of Praise* and wanted to meet me. They lived in a village called Marnhull, about forty miles from the college, and despite the fact that the husband had very poor health having had both legs amputated, they showered me with their love, fellowship and lots of lovely food. Their home became very special to me and I returned to college truly refreshed and blessed.

In January, at the beginning of the second term, my tutor, Stephen Dray, expressed his concern at the work that I was doing. Not that I did not do enough, but that I had to do so much! He realised that in comparison to the other students, I had to work much longer to produce the same work. I shrugged, but told him that I had accepted the situation as normal.

'College life should consist of more than simply writing out essays,' he said. 'There should be social interaction with fellow students and a lot more relaxation than you seem to be getting.'

I assured him that I felt learning and completing the work to be more important than socialising and that since I had to write with my toes, I just had to accept that it would all take me longer.

'Can you use a typewriter keyboard with your toes?' he asked me.

'Yes,' I said. 'I used to use a Possum typewriter, and the keyboard is more or less the same as a normal one, but it still takes me a long time to get all my notes in order.'

'But what about a computer word-processor?' he said. 'I'm sure it would reduce the amount of time you spend in writing essays. Many of the other students use them.'

I seriously considered this option for the next few months

until I went home for the Easter vacation, and then contacted Mr Davies, the Director of Education (responsible for education on the politically independent Isle of Man). He proved very supportive of my request and was confident that the Board would supply me with a word-processor – especially as I was paying the college tuition fees myself. Within minutes he had called a member of staff into his office from the computer department, requesting him to leave what he was doing and go with me to the shopping centre to order a computer. Amazed at their kindness, I could only ponder that this kind of help could probably only happen in an island community. Somehow the people are drawn together in a kind of close comradeship not possible on the mainland.

Within two days I had the word-processor at home on the floor of my bedroom where I practised with the keyboard and tried to grasp the computer language ready for my return to college after the Easter break. Back at college I could hardly believe the difference the computer made to my productivity. As my two big toes got more practised, all I had to do was type in all the relevant material on the given subject, then move words, sentences, paragraphs, and even whole pages if I wished, and the essay formed before my eyes. Before this, if I needed to change any part of what I had written, I had to use copious amounts of correction fluid, or write out the whole page – and even the whole essay, all over again. But now, when I was satisfied with what I had written, I simply pressed a key and, *hey presto*! the essay printed out, ready for submission to my lecturer! Suddenly I could produce a 2,500-word essay in a fraction of the time it had taken before. What a fantastic invention and how grateful I felt to Mr Davies and the Board of Education for providing it for me.

Now I could spend more time in recreational activities with

the other students, and I made use of every opportunity. One of the best happened twice each term when my tutor group, led by Stephen Dray and his wife Anne, arranged for us all to have an evening out together simply enjoying ourselves as a group. We might go into the New Forest for a walk, or perhaps have a meal, or maybe go ten-pin bowling. This disappointed me a little because the balls were too heavy for me to wield with my feet, but I loved skittles, which was very popular at the time in that part of the country. Volleyball was another matter. With a volley-ball court in the college grounds, we could play whenever we had any free time, and since I have never been a spectator when it comes to sport, I joined in as often as possible. In a way similar to when I played games at home with my family and friends as a child, the students altered the rules to allow me to chip the ball over the net with my feet. So I threw myself into the game – literally – as I headed the ball, dived, slid and flung my legs high in the air to get the best shots. I loved the exercise, athleticism and the competitive edge to the game, and had a wonderful time.

After a few weeks, however, we had to curb our enthusiasm a little following a reprimand from the student 'reps' who had the duty of monitoring behaviour in our activities. Apparently some people, they said, were being too competitive on the volleyball court and they felt that we needed to take a more relaxed view of the game. I must confess that I was one of the culprits. I enjoyed it enormously and the game often became quite aggressive when crucial match points became imperative. I resolved to try and remember that it was a game, and only a game, as we had been requested.

Each morning from Monday to Friday before lectures began a short service of worship would be held in the chapel. It was always a very precious time during which there were many highlights. One of them, however, has remained fresh in my memory to this day. Two lecturers, John Davies and Robin Wood, had recently returned from a summer vacation to Thailand and South Korea where millions were giving up their idol worship and turning to God. John and Robin were both profoundly changed by their experience and shared with us for about fifteen minutes how God's Holy Spirit was moving in South Korea.

John told us that he had been deeply touched by the earnestness of the Korean prayer life, and how he had gone to all-night prayer meetings where they literally had to climb over people at 2.00 a.m. to get to the main prayer room.

'Oh, to see this in Britain!' he grieved, and as we listened we were convicted about our somewhat blasé attitude to sin and our relationship to God. The powerful talk reduced us all to silence as John sat down. Then, from the silence, one student got up, walked to the front of the chapel and confessed to us all that he had used the photocopier without paying for its usage. This opened the floodgates and soon an orderly stream of students poured forward to confess specific wrongs with many tears, and to ask forgiveness. In the ensuing emotion-packed time, relationships were healed and restored, and continued to be healed during the next few weeks within the college and even further afield.

Neither did I escape the watershed. In that charged atmosphere, God spoke to me clearly about a bad attitude I held for the lecturer in speech, doctrine and church history. It stemmed back to the initial lectures she gave to us in my first year. I had been very sensitive about a remark made concerning correct speech and accents, and being very proud of my Irish roots and brogue, I took offence. Consequently I did not co-operate with what I saw as 'stupid' exercises. I maintained that God had given me the Irish accent of which I was very proud and since it had

never been a barrier before in sharing with others, I felt unlikely
– and unwilling – to change. That spark of anger affected all the
rest of her lectures even though I loved church history and I had
to admit that she was a very good lecturer.

After the convicting talk from John, I could not let the
situation go on. I went to my lecturer and apologised for my
attitude and for being half-hearted in her lectures. Thankfully, I
found the load lifted from my shoulders and as a consequence
really began enjoying learning about the great characters I
admired so much. From now on I noticed that the lecturer was
so enthused that I found myself enthused too! She really seemed
to ignite us! I looked back to my foolish 'pigheaded' Ulster
mindset which nearly spoiled my being challenged and blessed
through this particular lecturer's teaching.

Another area with which I had to come to terms occurred
during the homiletics (or preaching) class. Here all students, both
male and female, were required to preach to their colleagues for
fifteen minutes. Before coming to Moorlands I had never before
heard a woman preach, and now I was confronted by something
which would never be tolerated in my native Northern Ireland.
This could not be an issue that I could overcome easily – not so
much because of the preaching, but as a matter of *authority*. I
shared my natural apprehensions as the course of classes progressed, but as each woman performed her required exercise, a
few more bricks from my wall of prejudice came down.

Perhaps through the ages the men have so often been lazy
and disobedient to God's call to the ministry that now he has
raised up women who have faithfully responded and served in
the mission fields throughout the world, having to use all the
gifts of a pastor. Could it be, therefore, that in so many churches,
where women are relegated to making the tea and washing up,
we are losing out on many God-given talents and gifts?

Throughout my years at Moorlands I found myself challenged by all kinds of difficult subjects, many of which we were required to face and consider. One of them affected me in particular since it concerned the matter of abortion with special reference to the problem of disability. I formed part of an ethics presentation to the rest of the class which became so charged with emotion that several married students whose wives were pregnant had to leave. Of course, we had not intended this to happen, but the subject is so complex and emotive that no one could fail to be affected by it. Personally, the terrifying fact is that if I had been conceived after the Abortion Act of 1967, then I would almost certainly not have been allowed to live beyond a few months in the womb. My faith and convictions tell me that each individual is unique and equally valuable in God's sight, no matter what their physical or mental condition.

For each year of our course we were assigned to a local church with whom we would worship and get involved in any way relevant. In my first year I joined with four other students to attend a church in Parkstone, Poole, as part of an evangelism project. This was a well-established church with a lot of able members, but we helped wherever possible, in particular with door-to-door evangelism – a notoriously difficult exercise, but often blessed of God. I also had the opportunity to share my testimony for an hour with thirty teenagers, challenging them about their commitment to God. The placement taught us a lot about tackling difficult situations, relationships with existing church members and our position as helpers to an established church.

The second year offered a completely different situation as I helped in a newly 'planted' church in Charminster, Bournemouth. The church had been set up from its 'mother' church in Winton, and members consisted of people from

Winton who lived in the Charminster area. The new church opened on 10 September 1989, and I arrived on 24 September! My aims here were to experience being part of a small leadership team, to learn evangelism strategy and to observe generally what life in an 'embryo' church is like. The members welcomed us with open arms and we eagerly pitched into the work of making the new church known throughout the district.

In year three the Director of Pastoral Studies, Tim Marks, recommended that I do my 'pastoral placement' at St John's Church, Wimborne, Dorset, where the congregation reached around 550 members. As a large proportion of the members were elderly, I took on some of the home visiting – another new area for me to experience. In such a large church, the vicar kindly gave me plenty of opportunities to try all kinds of ministry: young children, teenagers, men's breakfasts, ladies' meetings, preaching, prayer and praise gatherings and lots more.

I found all these varied meetings rather daunting, but none so much as the classes and Christian Union meetings I was required to take in some of the more exclusive fee-paying private schools – a good number of which can be found around the Bournemouth area. On two consecutive mornings I nervously arrived at one of these schools, ready for an 8.00 a.m. start, and made my way to the beautiful but ancient college chapel. Before long the boys (there were very few girls) began to file in. Soon a sea of smartly uniformed young people sat waiting attentively, while their teachers, dressed in full regalia of caps and gowns, occupied the choir stalls like so many judges waiting to hear the case against the accused!

I took my prescribed place high up in the ornate pulpit, feeling like the defendant, and with my knees shaking I began my talk. I preached a humble message from 1 Corinthians 2, considering as I spoke that the sea of faces below me represented the future generation of lawyers, doctors, politicians and scientists. I reminded myself that they, too, needed to hear the wonderful message of Jesus Christ and his forgiveness, and I pressed on more confidently.

A special outreach in October 1989 offered me yet another first-time opportunity, when the entire Moorlands student body of 210 was invited to work alongside the churches of Tunbridge Wells, Kent, for a nine-day mission. Two weeks prior to our going, I was suddenly asked to step in and lead the team of ten students allocated to St James' Church. Unfortunately the original team leader's wife had a difficult birth of their first child, and he had to drop out of the mission. I felt rather overawed as several of my team had university degrees and, I was sure, could surpass me in organisational ability. God reminded me that all this did not matter one iota to him – it only mattered that I should obey. I therefore got on with the job and was amazed how encouragingly the team pulled together. In two weeks we had a comprehensive programme of activities prepared and were anxious to get on with the job.

One of our tasks was to take an after-school club at St James' Church. The vicar had told me that usually forty to fifty children attended regularly. In the event, I was unnerved to find ninety-three children there on the first day, followed thereafter by an attendance of about 130 each day! We had to run round early on Tuesday to the local shops for loads more badges, pencils, sweets and labels as prizes!

I had to take responsibility for one of the children's workshops. As usual, I made full use of my uniqueness to attract their attention by giving them demonstrations of me using my feet. I put a bowl of Smarties on the floor and then showed them how I held a spoon in my toes to pick up the Smarties and get them to my mouth. Then I put a piece of string across two chairs and showed how I could hang out washing by squeezing the pegs in my toes and pegging it on and off the line. Finally, I showed them how I could read a newspaper with my toes.

Then it was the children's turn. Mayhem reigned as thirty-five kids took off their shoes and socks and had a go with their toes. We had ten bowls of Smarties, dozens of pegs and several newspapers! The laughter and excitement as they endeavoured to succeed cannot be described! Interestingly, only one or two kids were able, with a little cheating, to get a Smartie into their mouths on the Monday, whereas by Thursday and Friday the later groups (who had been 'tipped off') were much more successful. They had been practising at home!

All our different placements and field studies provided us with many and various new experiences and opportunities. Some were eagerly tackled and gave a great deal of satisfaction; others proved more taxing and sometimes frustrating. But all were necessary and gave us valuable insights into Christian service in many areas. Although I had no real idea of what I wanted to do when my college course ended, I expected that God would lead me into some kind of Christian work which would absorb all my energies and take up most of my time. During the summer vacation at home on the Isle of Man in my second year at Moorlands, however, something was to happen which set me thinking in quite another direction.

When a team of young people went from our church, Broadway Baptist, to work alongside churches in Ireland, I looked forward to the visit enormously. Some time before, as I described in Chapter 9, a team had come to Broadway under the auspices of Baptist Youth Evangelism, an organisation that arranged for young people to give short-term help to needy churches. It had the double purpose of providing a church with the kind of help which it might not otherwise get, and it also gave the young people valuable experience in Christian work. The BYE team having helped us when we most needed a helping hand, it was suggested that now we might like to reciprocate by sending a team to offer a couple of weeks' help to churches in Ireland.

In fact, we sent two teams: one to Southern Ireland, and one to the north. I was part of the northern team based at Sion Mills Baptist Church near Strabane, County Tyrone, helping with two weeks' outreach. We stayed in the homes of church members, and each day we would mobilise for a planned exercise in evangelisation around the town. Then at mealtimes we gathered together in the church hall for a debriefing and to have our meals which had been prepared by a team of volunteers. One of these volunteers, Eunice, attracted my attention immediately. Shy and efficient and with a wonderful smile, she seemed to stand out from all the rest as she hurried about serving lunch to the hungry workers. I could hardly take my eyes from her. She seemed quite different from any girl I had seen before. I determined to speak to her at the first opportunity.

My heart skipped a beat when she seemed just as eager to speak to me, and before long we found ourselves longing for the brief times when we would meet up for meals or some other moment during each day. I discovered that she was a nurse in the nearby town of Omagh, and that she contemplated going back to college to do a midwifery course.

I began to dread the end of the visit. I could not bear the thought of returning to college in England, leaving Eunice miles away in Northern Ireland. In the short time since we met she had become a very special friend. When leaving day finally arrived, we agreed to write and keep in touch by telephone, but we would definitely not say 'goodbye' forever. Soon we would arrange a time when we could be together – not with all the others around but on our own so that we could talk.

It was hard to concentrate on my college work. Eunice's face kept invading my thoughts and my heart ached to see her. Again my days were punctuated by the times when I could hear her voice – albeit only by telephone. As the summer vacation approached, we made plans for a holiday together, and decided upon a tour of the West Coast of Eire. In this beautiful part of Southern Ireland, we could drive around the isolated lanes enjoying the scenery and being with each other.

I was ecstatic with joy at meeting Eunice again, and could hardly believe we were going to be able to spend two whole weeks more or less alone. It would be a wonderful time of getting to know each other better, although to me it seemed as though we had known each other all our lives.

As we travelled around the countryside, my mind went into overtime. It was increasingly clear that Eunice enjoyed my company and that we got on well together. I believed that nothing happened to us by accident or coincidence and that God had therefore brought us together. Could it be that at last I had met the one girl with whom I could spend my life? Over the years I had often been aware of the respect and admiration many women held for me regarding the way I had come to terms with my disability, and yet I longed for something more. I felt that I had a capacity for loving and being loved by one very special lady, and looked forward to the time when God would bring us together. Had that time come at last?

Again my heart skipped a beat at the thought, but it was swiftly followed by a sinking feeling as I remembered that life with me would not be quite so easy for a woman as it might be if I had two arms. For the first time I felt a twang of regret. Could I think of asking Eunice to marry me when she would inevitably have more responsibility for the practical things in our home? I tenaciously clung to the insistence that I could do anything that anyone else could do given time and practice, but in my heart of hearts I had to admit that life would not be *just* as simple as it might be if I had arms. As each day of the idyllic holiday passed, I talked more specifically about the future and what it might hold for us both.

Throughout my life I have battled with the problem as to whether other people can look beyond the lack in my physical appearance and see the true Brian. In childhood years I had to convince other children that I could do anything they could do – only I did it differently. But when I needed employment, the problem came more sharply into focus. I was confronted with a world where only the visibly 'normal' would do. Convincing prospective employers that I could be just as efficient as anyone with arms proved an uphill climb. But a close relationship with a woman seemed to be an even more uncertain question.

I recalled how on several occasions well-meaning Christian friends had tried to arrange for a single lady to sit with me at one of the Sunday lunches. Other Christians suggested finding another thalidomide girl for me! Yet others had offered the opinion that perhaps I should remain single, but I longed for the companionship and love of just one woman. I prayed that God would reveal his purposes to me and help me to accept it – whatever it might be.

The dreaded day of our holiday's end arrived. I had made my feelings for Eunice plain, but she seemed to be a little overwhelmed by my aspirations. Naturally, she did not want to rush into anything, and she reminded me that we both had college courses to finish, and probably a career to establish. She felt that the time was not right for launching a commitment to each other, and that we ought to wait for a while. Perhaps the enforced break as we returned to our courses would give us a chance to assess the situation and find out what the future held for us.

Back at home on the Isle of Man, my heart ached. I wondered if I would ever see my precious Eunice again. But she had promised to keep in touch, so I would have to be content with that for the time being. I took myself off to a quiet place beside the Injebreck Reservoir and, sitting on the embankment, I stared at the water in front of me. Its calm, peaceful surface contrasted with the turmoil within me.

'Lord, how I long for calm and peace just like that water,' I prayed, and although it took me some time to understand, I know that God began a healing work in me from that time. I would leave the whole thing in his hands, knowing that he only wanted the best for both Eunice and me. I would have to curb my impetuosity and await his timing. He had work for us both to do, and we must be obedient to his calling.

14

To the city

Some time before I went to Bible college, I found myself challenged by a passage of Scripture in Isaiah 58:

> If you spend yourselves on behalf of the hungry
> and satisfy the needs of the oppressed,
> then your light will rise in the darkness,
> and your night will become like the noonday.
> The Lord will guide you always;
> he will satisfy your needs in a sun-scorched land
> and will strengthen your frame.
> You will be like a well-watered garden,
> like a spring whose waters never fail.

As I read the words and allowed them to sink into my spirit, I felt God speaking to me.

'Brian, I want you to reach out to the helpless, the hopeless, the weak, the "nobodies", with love and compassion.'

Eagerly, I responded with 'Yes, Lord, of course – but how? When? And where?'

At Moorlands, the conviction that God wanted me to go in this direction increased. I read about the work of Jean Vanier who carried out an amazing ministry with the mentally handicapped, and I was profoundly challenged by one of his concepts that following the example of Jesus meant going 'down the career ladder' rather than up.

On Sunday evenings I often took a carload of friends to Lansdowne Baptist Church in Bournemouth. One particular Sunday, the minister, Steve Brady, spoke about his own life in Liverpool with regard to inner-city ministry.

'Life in the raw is found in the inner city!' he said. 'The desire to get up and leave is a phenomenon. This leaves the poor, the powerless, the old and the weak behind.'

The message impressed me deeply, and I added it to my already deep convictions. Then the next year, during my placement with St John's, Wimborne, I read the biography of Lord Shaftesbury whose ancestral home lay in the Wimborne area. His inspiring story touched me deeply, and I remembered Steve Brady's words. God surely must be directing me towards work with the needy. In 1991, therefore, as the end of my three years at college approached, I sent off for an application form to the Shaftesbury Society in London, where they had vacancies for urban link workers. A week later I was offered the opportunity of working with one of their churches in west London, together with another student from London Bible College, Andy Gilroy. On 3 September 1991, I arrived tired and stiff after the long journey from the Isle of Man to Brentford, London, where the pastor and his wife greeted me warmly together with my co-worker, Andy.

Our intended accommodation having fallen through,

eventually Andy and I together with the previous year's worker, Jill, found a house that we could share. It could not have been more of a contrast from my home in the tranquil Isle of Man. Here, two miles from Heathrow Airport and 500 metres from the M4 motorway, noise tore into every moment. As jets accelerated for take-off and roared overhead, the traffic on the motorway added a continual bombardment of reverberating noise that shook every building around. I wondered if I would be able to cope with it. How could anyone sleep in such an environment? How did people live with this constant intrusion of noise? I thought of the joyful days Eunice and I had spent in the peacefulness of Southern Ireland. I had had such hopes for our future, and yet now here I was, battling with the cacophony of inner London.

I would not give up, though. God had sent me here, and he would enable me to cope. It was to be several months before the noise ceased to be all encompassing and receded into the background.

Andy and Jill soon bought me a high stool for my birthday so that I could do my share of the washing up, and life settled into a routine. However, I was to discover one or two unexpected aspects of living in urban London. To begin with I found that I had to acquire a different attitude to driving. With so much traffic clogging every street, it became clear that the 'laid back' driver would get nowhere. Drivers who took their time and tried not to become stressed by the pressures all around them seemed to attract nothing but aggression from the frantic commuters. I quickly learned to be alert at all times, with an awareness of what the other road users might do. It made for very tiring driving, and I understood something of why stress plays such a part in people's lives in London. Sometimes I would use the underground trains to get around the city, but since they were often jam-packed with people, I really needed arms to hang on with. Any sudden start or stop would fling me against someone else or straight on to the floor.

Another unexpected discovery left me unsure whether to be glad or sorry! The area where Andy, Jill and I lived had a high Asian population, many of whom ran small shops. I willingly took my turn at doing the shopping or getting the occasional takeaway meal, but I was not prepared for what happened. I would get to the till with perhaps twenty-five pounds worth of food, only to find the owner refuse to take my money! When I protested he would explain that his principles did not allow him to take money from the disabled. His culture, he explained, demanded that he take care of the less fortunate in the community. I did not know quite how to handle the situation, but Andy and Jill declared that I would have to do the shopping from then on!

I found exactly the same situation when my computer printer broke down. I took it in a bag hung round my neck to a shop where the owner repaired the burnt-out micro-chip but insisted he wouldn't dream of charging anything for the work! Normally I would have agreed whole-heartedly with the excellent morals of helping the weak and disadvantaged, but I considered myself in neither category, so had no idea how to react!

The church in which we were centred was situated in the part of the estate where the council housed all their problem families. My first reaction on seeing the church building was that it resembled a fortress. It had a brick wall to keep people out; the windows were covered with steel mesh and everything movable was fastened by padlocks and bolts.

I realised immediately that unless I quickly drew the local youth on to my side, my car would probably find itself jacked up minus four wheels in no time. Tactics demanded that I once again shamelessly flaunt my disability in order to attract their attention and claim their interest. As expected, they were flabbergasted at how I could drive without arms, and during that first week I employed myself in taking groups of youngsters for a spin around the estate. My aim achieved, I hoped it would secure a safe passage for my car – and me – in the months to come.

It was not long before I saw the desperate state of all the local inhabitants around us. Most lived in indescribably atrocious squalor, with the elderly confined like prisoners in their homes with fear inscribed on their faces because of constant muggings. I understood what was meant by the city being described as a 'concrete jungle' where only the fittest survive. These desperate people welcomed me into their homes, and over a cup of tea poured out their longing hearts. Oh, how much they needed to know the love of God in their lives! And how insignificant I felt my weak efforts to be! When I returned to my car, often I would sit in despair, crying to God.

Now and again, however, glimmers of hope broke through the wall of darkness as I found one or two of these dear folk who trusted God against all the odds. Peace and hope radiated from their faces as they told me stories of his goodness and faithfulness. I began to realise what a privileged position I have always enjoyed with a secure home both at school and with my family, and in beautiful places. All my life I had been unaware that I possessed the priceless gift of freedom of choice. I could choose where I lived or worked; what I ate; what I wore, and much, much more. But here in the city the poor, elderly and the disabled, the single parents and the mentally ill had never heard of Jesus – other than as a swear-word – and they often had no choice and no voice to speak for them. I knew that at Christmas I would be going home to the tranquillity of the Isle of Man to recharge my body, mind and spirit, whereas these people I tried to serve had no other world but the one in which they existed.

In the New Year I anticipated returning home during my week's leave for Easter, but before that, in March, I was due a weekend's break which I had planned to spend in London. However, all my plans changed when I received a letter from home which mentioned that George Verwer of the youth missionary organisation Operation Mobilisation would be speaking on the Isle of Man during that very weekend. Having heard him at college a few years earlier, I was impressed by his vision and enthusiasm, and very keen to hear him again. So I determined to drive home in spite of the long journey. I expected to be enthused by George's message, but I did not expect the suggestion he made when I spoke to him after the meeting.

'There's a conference in Holland in two weeks' time,' he told me. 'It aims to accelerate awareness and outreach to the disabled in the community, and to provide training and networking opportunities for those with a ministry to the disabled. Joni Eareckson Tada is the speaker, and I'm sure you would be encouraged by what she has to say. Do you think you could manage to get there?'

I had read Joni's inspirational story of the tragic swimming accident that left her a paraplegic, and how after many months of depression she finally allowed God to change her life by using her just as she was. She now had an international ministry including her talent in mouth painting and singing, to reach out to disabled people everywhere.

'But I have to go back to London to work,' I said. 'I don't know whether I can get time off for something like that.'

'I would willingly pay for you to go,' said George, to my

astonishment. 'See what you can do. Get a global perspective, Brian!'

His enthusiasm inspired me to make an attempt at least, although I had never considered that my ministry could be to the disabled. Back in London, to my surprise, my pastor agreed that I could have the time off, providing it was taken as holiday, so within two weeks I found myself on the way to Holland!

Right from the start I was swept up in the wonderful enthusiasm of people from all over the world. Even as I waited in the airport lounge, two Americans, Bill and Christopher, introduced themselves to me and explained that they with twenty-six others had been invited to pray around the clock for three days during the conference. Excitement mounted as I listened to them, because for about four years my heart had become burdened to pray for others.

Directly after registration Bill took me to the 'Upper Room' where I met Joni herself. Here was a lady who had arms – and legs – yet could not use them. Although she had been confused and distressed when the accident that robbed her of movement first happened, she had become convinced that God had arranged for her to be this way so that she could work more effectively for him. Similarly, I knew that my lack of arms did not prevent God from using me in his service, because all he required was a life given over to him.

Thrilled to be with all these eminent and dedicated people, I drank in all I could, experiencing during the next few days a whole new world of prayer. I joined in the round-the-clock prayer 'watches' and discovered that even the two-hour sessions during the night seemed like ten minutes as I lost myself in conversation with God! But I did not want to miss the seminars simply because I had been praying during the night! Bleary-eyed and exhausted, I made my way to the interpretation booths where the seminars were translated into English. I would not miss a minute!

As the few days drew to a close, I began to assess what I had learnt. The conference had centred on the need to include people with disabilities into all aspects of the life of the church. Joni had thrown out the challenge to minister to the disabled community, making the love of Christ truly accessible to all.

My personal opinion had always been that I was not 'disabled' – just unique. It did not really occur to me that I needed to *become* accepted in the church. Christ made me as I am – he certainly accepted me and he fits me for service. But what of others who may be unique in some way? Some did not enjoy the kind of confidence I had learned from a stable family life. Some were hurting and rejected. These were the people Christ needed us to reach. Could I be one of those whom God was calling to take up the challenge? Did God bring me to this conference to discover his will for my life?

I returned to my work in London tired, elated, but prayerfully thoughtful. At the moment I had a duty to take the love of God to the poor and needy of Brentford, and I set to the task with renewed vigour.

But when I reported back to the pastor, all did not seem well. He did not give me the encouragement I expected. It even seemed as though he did not agree with the way I worked. Then, to my consternation, he called me in to speak with him, and told me that his daughter would now be accompanying me on my visits and that all I would be required to do was ask the people I visited to fill in a questionnaire. I was told that I must stop sharing my faith.

I could hardly believe what I heard. Confused and puzzled, I cried to God again. 'Why am I here if I can't share the love and hope of God with these people?' I felt as though a rug had been pulled from under my feet and I could no longer stand.

With my ministry so curtailed, I discussed the position with a friend at the Shaftesbury Society headquarters. I explained that as the pastor and I were so different in our outlook, it would be better if I tendered my resignation at the end of the year in July. He suggested that perhaps I ought to stay and learn from my experiences instead. I went back resolved to fast and pray for God's guidance.

After a week of prayer and fasting during April, I became convinced that it would be mutually beneficial if I left my role as urban link worker at the end of July, and I reported this to the pastor. He accepted my resignation, and I felt a burden lift from my shoulders.

Then, true to God's perfect timing, I heard that my home pastor, David Gordon, was visiting London and would come to see me. In May, therefore, I shared my feelings and my situation with him. I knew that I had a lot to learn and that God had a purpose for bringing me to work in Brentford, but I had expected it to be a more fulfilling time. God had taught me many things and perhaps he would reveal more to me in the future, but for the moment I was confused and puzzled as to where he wanted me to go and what he wanted me to do.

'Well, Brian,' David said thoughtfully, 'I don't know what God has in mind for you, but there's plenty of work for you to do at Broadway if you think it is right for you to come back when you leave here.'

This would give me time to assess my future and seek God as to what I should do next, and I gratefully accepted his offer. So in July I made my way back to the Isle of Man, glad to leave the noise of London for the peace of my beautiful Island home.

I had arranged with David that I would begin work at Broadway in September, so that I could take time in August for a holiday to restore my flagging spirits. On my first morning back at home it was wonderful to wake up to the familiar sounds of the Island instead of the roar of aircraft and traffic. I lay for a while listening to the chirping of sparrows and the cry of a seagull. A car or two drove by, the sounds rising to a crescendo and then dying away. I could even hear the footsteps of people on their way to work, and if I concentrated, I fancied I could just make out the sound of the sea ebbing and flowing on the shore. I told myself I had probably imagined it, but I determined to go for one of my usual walks along the headland at Bradda Head as soon as possible. I thought of all the dear people I had met in Brentford, waking to the barrage of noise and the insecurities of the inner city. My heart went out to them and I prayed that God would relieve their anxieties and stress, but I wondered the more at the goodness of God in bringing me back to my beloved island where he knew I would be happiest.

I met with David and the rest of the leadership team to discuss what my duties would be. We considered how best I could fit into the team. I did not rate myself as a preacher – not compared with David's gifted preaching – but assured them that I would make the effort if required to do so. Rather, I felt my gifts lay more in the pastoral sphere, discipling young Christians and in working with young people.

With church membership growing, there was plenty to do, so I soon had a busy schedule of visitation and helping with the youth club, fitting in any other tasks as required. But the growing church membership, though wonderful, gave us cause for concern. It had been growing at a rate of roughly thirty new members each year, and if it continued in this way, we would soon outgrow the available space. Even now the Sunday school had to be accommodated in the damp, dank basement, and the situation was becoming critical. David and the rest of the church leaders discussed the problem.

The church building was in such a bad state that we would really have liked to have moved somewhere else, but since our site was valueless with its confined space and limited use, we knew this would be impossible. After checks by a structural engineer, we heard that the building was, in fact, structurally sound, so radical changes would have to be made instead.

Before long, detailed plans were submitted to the council. The vastly expensive project would provide us with a completely new floor dividing the church so that additional Sunday school rooms would be available, together with extensive renovation. Everything decided, we decided to push on to get the job completed before the church's centenary the next year, in May 1993. But God's plans were better than ours.

During July the fellowship had courageously purchased two adjacent buildings. Early in August I arrived back on the Island after leaving the small church in London. David enthusiastically welcomed me home.

'Come with me,' he said. 'I want your opinion of something.' We left the church but did not go far. Adjacent to the church stood two large five- or six-storey hotels that had seen better days. They had been closed for some time, and had been deteriorating steadily. David led me, mystified, up the steps of the first building. We went in through the front door with its peeling paint and stood in the hallway. The plaster crumbled from the walls, the floorboards were holed, and the windows smashed. It felt damp and cold.

'Well,' said David, cautiously, 'can you imagine what these places would look like if they were done up – or,' he paused, 'maybe gutted and rebuilt inside?'

I looked. The task would be gargantuan. Anyway, what had it got to do with us?

'We've got them for a very good price – as property goes – and although a lot of work has to be done on them they would provide us with all the rooms we need, wouldn't they?' He went on, a quizzical look in his eye, 'Not only could they house the Sunday school, but we could expand our work with the local community. Do you reckon we could take on a renovation project with these two hotels? You are pretty good at seeing things how they *could* be – what do you think?'

Straight away my natural optimism switched into gear and I could see what he meant. 'Certainly,' I said, 'it would be wonderful to have so much accommodation. We could really make a contribution to the community, I'm sure.' My mind, like David's, jumped ahead to the many excellent projects that could be achieved given the right premises. But it would not be easy. 'What about the cost?' I brought us both down to earth. 'It would be astronomical. We could do a lot of it ourselves, of course, but even so, it would take a lot of money to complete.'

'God can do it,' said David, confidently.

And so, after much prayer and discussion, the original plans for the church renovations were changed. They would still be carried out, but in a slightly lesser form, bearing in mind the new accommodation that we would eventually have in the two hotels.

From then on, money began to come in from committed members and in other wonderful gifts as we prayed for God's provision. Arrangements were made for us to use the local leisure centre and high school for services while work continued on the church, and the plans began to take shape. There would be little free time for me over the next few years.

15

Korea!

Towards the end of 1992 I received an unexpected letter from a dear friend, Doralee Vanfossen from Pittsburg, USA, whom I had met at the conference in Holland. It was good to hear from her again, and to read the encouragement to prayer that she included. Further on in her letter, however, she mentioned a conference to be held in South Korea in October 1993 – The 14th Church Growth International Conference – and that she had put my name forward to be a delegate! My immediate reaction was to laugh and say, 'Impossible!' – not only concerning the cost, but more so for the practical difficulties arising through having no arms. But as I thought the prospect over, my mind went back to the day in the college chapel when Robin had shared his experiences in Korea. What an amazing opportunity! How could I refuse? I had got over difficulties before – I could get over them again! I excitedly made arrangements to join the conference.

During the next three months doubts began filtering through my mind. The extreme distance to travel; the language barrier to overcome and, yes, maybe I wouldn't be able to cope. And then I heard that another friend from the previous conference, Bill Anderson from Colorado Springs, USA, would be the assistant co-ordinator of the Gideon's Army of Intercessors at Seoul. I would know at least two people there. God had provided contacts and friends for me. I would not be entirely alone. I needed no more encouragement. God required me to keep an appointment with him in Seoul, in October 1993.

When the day arrived, David, my pastor, drove me the eight miles to the airport, left my luggage and said his farewells, assuring me of his and the church's prayers. At this time on a Friday evening there were always several flights to the mainland, and I soon heard my flight to Heathrow announced. Due to refurbishment taking place at the airport, all passengers were escorted through the same gate and across the wet, windy tarmac to the aircraft. The stewardess showed me to my seat, but to our surprise it was taken. Another seat was found and as this part of the journey would only be fifty-five minutes it did not matter to me anyway. I asked the stewardess to fasten my seat belt, then another stewardess offered me a boiled sweet. This I gratefully accepted as it usually helped me with the high-altitude problem with my ears, and I settled back to await take-off. Within a few minutes the announcement came: 'We are about to take off for Birmingham . . .'

'Oh no!' I gasped, and shouted out, 'I'm for London, Heathrow!' My blushes were saved to some extent when another passenger shouted out the same thing, and we were quickly rushed off to another plane which was all ready with engines roaring. With just enough time for another boiled sweet, we lifted from the runway.

Beside me sat a Muslim businessman from Khartoum, Sudan. He had been to the Isle of Man for just one day and as we took off he prayed for Allah's protection. It was a good opportunity for me to share my faith in Christ Jesus, and he listened respectfully.

On arrival at Heathrow, I made my way to the home of two friends, Julie and Trevor, whom I had known from my time in Brentford, and enjoyed renewing our friendship as I stayed there overnight. The next morning, bright with autumn colour after the wind and rain of the night before, Trevor carried my luggage to the train which would take me back to Heathrow and the second leg of my flight, this time to Schipol, Amsterdam.

The final part to Seoul was to be a thirteen-hour flight, which I expected to find rather confining in the closely fitted seats. I was therefore surprised to find myself allocated one of eight seats which had double the legroom of any others! My feet being my 'hands', this meant I had more room to move and get comfortable without inconvenience to other passengers. I had also remembered to wear a shirt that did not need tucking in so that I would look presentable on the flight when I no doubt would have to make several visits to the toilet. I was very glad to find that the seat next to me on the right was unoccupied. Being left-footed, this became a great help particularly when eating because I could swing my left leg naturally with comfort and ease – amazing neighbouring passengers with my dexterity!

We landed at Kimpo International Airport at 10.30 a.m. on Sunday morning. I had not slept at all since leaving Julie and Trevor's house. Adrenaline and excitement kept me going non-stop. As I stepped out into the streets of Kimpo pushing my luggage in a trolley with my chest, the noise and confusion of the city mixed with the language barrier met me full force. In my ignorance, the taxi I chose happened to be one of the most expensive, but I eventually arrived at the Yoido Full Gospel Church, Seoul. Here I watched in total amazement as ushers held back a throng of 60,000 eager worshippers. My only experience of such vast numbers had occurred when I went to cheer on my favourite football team: Manchester United at Old Trafford! Here, the people flocked to meet with Jesus Christ. Suddenly I found myself surrounded by a fast-moving sea of beaming faces, saints of God who were all streaming toward the main sanctuary that held 32,000, with services relayed to adjacent buildings and the Education and World Mission Centre which held another 30,000. All this happened *seven* times each Sunday with six additional services during the week! No wonder Robin had been so affected by the scene, and sad for our own Christless society.

Seeking out the registration office on the twelfth floor of the World Mission Centre building, I could not find words to describe seeing so many people crammed into rooms, corridors or any available space where they could see a television monitor relaying the services. The hunger for God left me speechless. My mind swept back to our own church with its need for more room with good Sunday school and other facilities. Here in Seoul, thousands of little ones were taught in groups of a dozen or so in corridors and corners, while others sat outside under trees, on the grass and even on the pavement.

At the registration office, Miss Lee spoke to me in English and after a welcoming chat directed me to the 1.00 p.m. service. I could so easily have put my head down and slept, but Miss Lee seemed so enthusiastic, I could not help but take up her suggestion. She told me that it would take just thirty minutes for the sanctuary to empty and refill – 32,000 people were trained to exit the building in ten minutes so that another 32,000 could take the next twenty minutes to seat themselves. The sheer scale and organisation of it all took my breath away! I made my way to the special balcony area where overseas visitors could sit and listen to the speaker in their own language through headphones. Most languages of the world were catered for – especially if they were given advance warning.

The service is one I will never forget. I was so physically tired, yet God refreshed my spirit through the praise of the massed singing. Asking my neighbour to remove my headphones for me, I was deeply touched by the fervency and faithfulness of these people who sought the Lord in prayer, seemingly oblivious to everyone around them. Their humility and enthusiasm, and their love for God profoundly moved me.

Then Pastor Yonggi Cho got up to preach – as he does three times every Sunday, leaving the associate pastors to take the other services. In spite of my tiredness I listened, spellbound. I had heard and read so much of this great man, and yet I never thought I would hear him 'in the flesh'. He spoke about the humanity and humility of Jesus Christ as he served his disciples by washing their feet. The message was touching and relevant, and we left the meeting challenged, humbled and inspired.

I set to finding my accommodation for the forthcoming week. It turned out to be a one-hour journey from Seoul, up in the mountains – the International Prayer and Fasting Mountain, to be precise. I later learned that this was one of over two hundred places of prayer in the mountains throughout South Korea.

Our journey took us along the Han River embankment where people indulged in an array of activities: tennis, volleyball, archery, fishing, football and other sports unfamiliar to me. Then on through the picturesque countryside covered in early morning frost, and on up to the mountains. The spectacular scenery reminded me of Switzerland – breathtaking in its beauty with awesome, sawtooth rock cliffs covered with ice caps. The rural landscape spread out before me, brilliant with its orchards of brilliant yellows and vivid reds, and with green rice-planted fields being harvested as late as October.

Only later in my stay was I told that the prayer mountain lay very close to the United States' demilitarised zone which divides the nation at roughly the thirty-eighth parallel, and that we were there at a time of heightened tension due to possible nuclear capability being realised in North Korea.

The prayer mountain retreat consisted of a chapel and a dormitory with 'western' accommodation – that is, furniture including beds – a canteen and a 10,000-seat sanctuary. In addition 250 prayer grottoes dotted the area.

I crashed into my bed as jet-lag and lack of sleep finally overcame me, and it would be another two days before my body adjusted to the time differences.

On Monday I had my first taste of real Korean food which included rice at every meal. I made a valiant attempt to eat my *tchigae* – a spicy stew of fish and vegetables – with chopsticks, but I did not quite have the dexterity needed to use them with my toes! Thankfully the locals, without any verbal explanation, came to my rescue by offering me a spoon; otherwise I would have been fasting for two weeks!

I discovered that on an average day, from seven in the morning to seven at night, three thousand people would arrive at the Prayer Mountain via an hourly shuttle coach service. And if room could not be found on a coach, then the people would find some other method of transport to get them there.

The prayer grottoes, each about four feet square, were built into the side of the hills. A door ensured privacy and a mat on which to kneel and pray provided the sole furnishing. One took one's own candle for light, and left shoes outside – to let others know that the grotto was occupied. Then a time of prayer lasting for several hours seemed to be normal.

At the main prayer sanctuary, people came direct from work

for a whole evening. Usually, the entire family together began with three-quarters of an hour of praise – children, parents and grandparents – and at the front of the sanctuary a large floor space allowed the first fifteen hundred people to bring their beds (a rolled up mat or sleeping bag), too, for the night! Such eagerness to spend time with God in prayer left me wondering and humbled.

During the evening many deacons, distinguished by wearing bright yellow sashes, would pray with individuals from their cell group. On one particular evening a deacon came and prayed with me. He spoke in Korean and I have no idea what he said, but tears flowed down my cheeks, and I felt God simply saying, 'Brian, I'm here, and I love you!' Although the language barrier prevented me from understanding the three-quarter-hour long sermons, I had no problem joining in with the praise, some of the songs being tunes I knew well. I was simply overwhelmed by God's love pouring out from my brothers and sisters up in the mountains. I can truly say, 'Here are a people who whole-heartedly seek after God and long to know him better.'

The banquet held for the seven hundred guests was an unforgettable experience. Held in the Education Centre, I found myself seated between a brother in Christ from India on my left and another from Nigeria on my right wearing his national garments in full splendour. There were so many courses – food, food and yet more food! I soon learnt that there are five basic tastes of Korean cuisine: sour, hot, bitter, sweet, and salty, and that they alternate between crisp and tender, dry and saucy, spicy and mild. As the meal progressed we laughed and teased each other about what we might be eating – could it have been octopus . . .? Thankfully, I found that all Korean food is cut into small pieces during preparation and is eaten with a spoon, or chopsticks. Looking round the room, I noticed with relief that I was not the only one passing on the chopsticks!

As the conference began in earnest, I searched for answers to my first questions. I could not help but wonder, '*Why* is God working in this wonderful way here in South Korea?' And '*How* did it all begin?' Pastor Yonggi Cho soon began to answer my questions. It had all started in Korea in the late 1950s with a handful of people in a disused US army tent on the embankment of the Han River. A few people had a vision and a dream of what God could do in their country, and they began to pray.

Now we were being challenged. 'Ask the Holy Spirit to give *you* the vision and the dreams,' Pastor Yonggi Cho enthused. 'Dreams for the places where God has placed *you*!' He went on to urge us to pray *specifically* for direction and blessing on our countries, and he reiterated that prayer was the mainstay of everything – *real, unreserved, whole-hearted prayer*. I remembered with shame that back home in the Isle of Man, I often struggled to get out of bed to go to the corporate monthly prayer meeting three minutes away in my car. In contrast, the people here gave up time, food and sleep in order to pray.

At one of the spectacular presentations held in the Olympic Stadium for the visiting delegates together with 175,000 Koreans, the prayer went on and on – two hours of praying together – whereas my prayers on a given topic ran out after ten minutes.

During the first week of my stay I had an opportunity to visit one of the 51,000 home ('cell') groups. These are the number one priority within the church in South Korea. In these small, friendly groups, both pastoral care and evangelism take place. Part of the gathering is the all-important but simple meal after the meeting. I learned that people were being reached for God through these meals. New people were invited to the weekly meal and began to enjoy the company, then were curious as to why everyone else arrived an hour earlier. Many would eventually decide to attend the hour's meeting, and they would discover God – and so the church grew. But the home groups did not exist merely to attract new members to the church. They provided essential pastoring to the people. Each week needs were met, hurts healed, joys and encouragements shared.

Soon after we arrived, I found myself to be the inadvertent cause of one lady's distress as tears poured down Jade Lim Jee Pang's cheeks. It transpired that thirty-one years earlier she had given birth to a little girl affected by thalidomide, and seeing me brought the trauma flooding back. The child survived only a few weeks, but Jade's husband abandoned her, leaving her no alternative but to turn to a convent for refuge. However, after some years, Jade had remarried happily and now had a grown-up family, but her friends in the home group had never heard her sad story before. We were all in tears, but glad that now Jade could receive the support and care she needed to help with the healing process.

The second week of the conference was to be spent in Seoul, so with some sadness I left my new friends on the prayer mountain retreat to travel to the big city. The registration point for this part of the conference was the magnificent Lotte Hotel, so expensive that it could be used only by the very rich. Four hundred delegates from forty-six nations began to gather together, ready for transfer to their allotted accommodation, and while I waited in the queue I idly read a tourist brochure and had a cup of Ginseng tea.

As usual, I did not wear shoes or socks, especially in this wonderful hotel with the deep pile carpets. To my amazement, however, suddenly the reception manager approached me with a frown and asked me to replace my shoes and socks in the public area! Quickly I explained the reason why I had to keep my toes free for use, and to my relief, he apologised profusely and graciously.

After the four-hour registration period, we boarded coaches that took us on to the Kwanglim Methodist Church, which had a congregation of 62,500 people over five services each Sunday. As we arrived, the church's choir accompanied by an orchestra sang to welcome us. It was a wonderful and touching start to the week. Then Pastor Sundo Kim introduced us to the church and its beginnings – again rising from nothing in the 1950s to the vast congregation now. My mind boggled at the church growth in Korea. Why could it not be done in our own country? We have the same unchangeable God . . . The amazing situation became all the clearer through a wonderful story about the church football team. Apparently it is called the 'Hallelujah Team', and one year they reached the final of the Korean equivalent of the FA Cup.

'Imagine the scene,' said the pastor. 'Suddenly the Hallelujahs scored a goal, and the whole stadium reverberated to the sound of "Hallelujah! Hallelujah!" '

I imagined the same thing happening in the Isle of Man for the 'Broadway Hallelujah Team'! Or even at Old Trafford! What a marvellous prospect!

We had been warned that our accommodation in this church's prayer mountain retreat would consist of large dormitories of men and women lying on mats on the floor. We had to admit that to our relief we discovered that the US Army had arranged for two hundred camp beds to be provided for the conference! It was good to meet up with Bill Anderson and others of the folk I had met before in Holland, and we renewed our friendships as we settled in.

With the emphasis so solidly on prayer here, no conference could go on without a full and committed prayer backing, and I was overwhelmed when Bill nominated me to be a participant in the seventy-strong prayer team. I had to fill in an application form that made me realise just how insignificant I was among all the 'giants' in the faith around me. The forms had obviously been designed to accommodate leaders in Christian work – great men and women with wide ministries – writers, preachers and ministers who represented whole nations, organisations or continents.

As I described myself as a simple 'church worker' and wrote 'none' in the spaces that asked for my publications and further ministries, I felt extremely small and inadequate. I battled with this feeling for a day or so, confiding my insecurity to Bill whom I knew would pray for me. Then, as I surveyed the glorious view across the valley from the prayer garden high up in the mountain, God reminded me of a simple fact. He listened not only to the prayers of the great and mighty, but also to the prayers of the small and insignificant. *Every* prayer was heard and valuable. He simply required *all* his people to pray. I remembered and rejoiced. What a wonderful privilege it was for me to be here! *My* prayers were important to God too. He had brought me here to carry out a task for him, and I would do it joyfully. I went back to the conference and set to organising my prayer team and the twenty-four hour 'prayer watch' to back up the work.

By the end of the second conference, my ears and heart were ringing with the volume of information and instruction I had heard, and I knew that I could never again be satisfied with the kind of complacent Christianity that is the hallmark of the West. In South Korea there are more than twelve million Christians making up 26 per cent of the population, and attending thirty thousand churches! And all of this has mushroomed since the 1950s. In Great Britain we struggle to achieve a fraction of this percentage, and even many of these are simply nominal Christians.

Like John Davies and Robin Wood who spoke to us at Moorlands Bible College about their Korean trip, I too felt very burdened that our country is so far from God. And like them, I returned home longing that the Korean experience might happen here and that God would be openly worshipped in our towns and villages as he is in the far-off country of Korea.

16

Looking to the future

My two-week experience in South Korea over, I now returned to the work – or rather, the *upheaval* – back at home! The church refurbishment had been finished by this time, and the congregation moved proudly into the gleaming new building. We would now be turning our attention to the hotels.

But in between all this, I began to feel that the time had come for me to make a further stand towards my independence. Up until now I had been living at home with my parents, but the prospect of having a home of my own attracted me.

It was therefore with a great deal of excitement I began to look at bungalows around Douglas and Onchan. But I would not do anything rash. In the same way that I had carefully researched the market with regard to my block of flats, I went about the business of looking for my home. It would probably be a 'once and for all' project because any bungalow – no matter how apparently suitable – would need to be adapted for my specific use. I did not want to make any mistakes, so I searched carefully and took note of all the pros and cons of every property I viewed.

Eventually I came across a plot of land only one mile away from my parents' home. After all I had seen, it seemed the most sensible thing to have a bungalow built to my own specification so that I could have everything in it arranged to my convenience. The bungalow soon took shape and as the walls grew, so did my excitement. I did often wonder if I had left anything important out in my instructions to the builder, but as far as I knew, there seemed to be nothing more I could need. My dad had enjoyed coming round to the bungalow with me to watch the progress, and as we looked, we sometimes thought of good practical ideas which we shared with the site foreman. He took our changes in good part and did not seem to be irritated by our suggestions, so I trust we did not cause him too much bother! I also remembered to ask that my garage be built four feet wider than usual – nothing to do with my driving, more to do with ease of access!

When moving-in day arrived – 17 November 1994 – Mum, Dad and I, with broad grins on our faces, all pitched in to get my new furniture settled. Then, tired but satisfied, Mum headed straight to the swivel rocking chair in the conservatory. What a delight it was for me to see her seated in my chair and in my house. Dad's delight, he declared, was to have all my books and my collection of ornamental eagles transferred from their house to mine. Maybe he would have room to rock in a chair of his own at last! I had been collecting ornamental eagles for some time because they were a symbol to me of what the Bible says in Isaiah 40:31: 'Those who hope in the Lord will renew their strength. They will soar on wings like eagles; they will run and not grow weary, they will walk and not be faint.' The eagle had always been special to me, and my collection had become very large. Moving them to my own home somehow seemed to reinforce the sentiments of that text.

Once settled, I turned my attention to the garden – well, to the area of bare ground around my bungalow! I had never really enjoyed gardening before, but now I discovered how relaxing it could be as I dug up the soil with my toes. Perhaps the many stones I removed inspired me, but soon I decided to build a rock garden with a water feature. My own stock of stones proved insufficient, however, so I made an offer my neighbours couldn't refuse – that of clearing their gardens, too, of rocks and stones.

Then with Mum and Dad seated in the conservatory watching the action, they could not suppress smiles as all shapes and sizes of rocks came flying over the fence! One neighbour later said that I was like a little JCB digger flicking tonnes of rocks with my toes.

I was grateful for these times with Dad in my own home because on New Year's Eve, just over a month later, Dad died in his sleep. In my grief I tried to remember that at least he had lived long enough to see me settled in a home of my own.

Having got my bungalow and garden arranged to my liking, I could now turn my attention back to the work that still went on at the church. Suddenly I had no spare time. When I wasn't carrying out my pastoral work, I could be found stripping and preparing walls, painting, or any other task I could reach with my toes – and I made sure not much passed me by! Until late every evening and every Saturday the work pushed ahead. It was great to see the plans taking shape, and I worked on, often exhausted, but with enthusiasm. Sometimes, however, I had to admit to some discouragement as I noticed yet again the same half a dozen or so of our growing congregation coming in to help.

'Where are all the rest?' I complained to David as we surveyed the extensive work yet to be done. 'We could get all this finished in half the time if all the able-bodied of the church would only do their share.'

'Yes,' replied David, guardedly, 'but you must remember that they are not all as free as you. Many have families to consider.'

It was true, of course. I could arrange my time to suit myself, but others had home commitments. I had no wife to go home to . . .

Over the next few years the two hotels were completely gutted and rebuilt inside. Gangs of members would spend much of their free time pulling down ceilings, ripping out walls and emptying loads of rubbish into skip after skip. It took over four years to complete the work. But finally on 21 February 1997, the Rev. John James, President of the Baptist Union of Great Britain, officially opened 'the Alpha Centre'. At the opening ceremony our people gathered to view the amazing transformation that had taken such dedication and hard work. We decided to use the word 'Alpha' as the name because it is the first letter of the Greek alphabet and is used in the Bible to describe God as the 'beginning' (together with 'Omega' – the end). We hoped that our beautiful new premises would be the *beginning* for many people; a place of 'new beginnings' where they could find solace, help and, most importantly, the love of God.

And so we praised God for all he had done for us in the provision of this new centre. Had most of the congregation known in the beginning that the whole project would have cost upwards of a quarter of a million pounds, they would have laughed the idea to scorn. But God can and does provide. And he had provided all the astronomical cost.

As the doors were opened, church members – together with those who had worked so hard over the previous four years to achieve this dramatic change – poured in to proudly survey their handiwork. Now we had all the room necessary to reach out to the community. We had ample space for the Sunday school, of course, but even more than that, a coffee and Christian bookshop offered somewhere for people to drop in from the street; counselling suites and prayer rooms provided havens where help could be given to those in need; offices and a committee room catered for the official business of the church; and right at the top of the building, a games room gave the young people somewhere to meet and have fun. In addition, several other Christian organisations made their bases in the building, so that the whole centre provided a comprehensive cover of help and outreach to anyone who cared to make use of it.

It is amazing to look back now and remember the two dozen or so who attended our church in the early days, and to see the two or three *hundred* who cram into the services now. Pastor David Gordon's vision was certainly justified as today's more than two-hour worship services ring to the sound of music from all kinds of instruments rather than just the organ as in the old days, and to the praises of the people.

However, God's work never finishes. The refurbished church and the Alpha Centre premises are not the end of the line. For the moment we concentrate on reaching out to the people of Douglas and the surrounding area and looking to bring them to a knowledge of a loving God. But who knows what plans God has for us in the future? We simply look to God and pray that any further work or developments will be to his glory as well as for the benefit of the community.

My own work now falls into a pattern of discipling young Christians, visiting and simply being a 'Barnabas' – that is, an 'encourager'. I am not happy to be a preacher, but prefer to work behind the scenes in any capacity God puts in my way. God, in his love, has provided me with a job I love and that suits my capabilities. But he has provided it in the place I love most – the beautiful Isle of Man. I would be willing to go wherever he wants me to be, but I am grateful for the opportunity to work for him in lovely surroundings.

I had heard very little from Eunice apart from Christmas cards each year, when suddenly in April 1996 I received a letter from her. My heart skipped a beat as I recognised her handwriting and, using my toes to rip open the letter, I read about her work in a military hospital in Saudi Arabia. I wrote back straight away, and from there we corresponded for a while, commiserating with each other over the recent deaths of both her father and mine. Just after Christmas that year we met up and had a wonderful time renewing our friendship after a six-and-a-half year gap. She returned to Saudi Arabia again and letters and phone calls followed at intervals during 1997. In July my hopes were at their highest when we relived the holiday in Southern Ireland that we enjoyed during the year of our meeting.

As we walked along the beach looking out on to the restless Atlantic Ocean, I carefully broached my future hopes, but I could tell that Eunice found it very hard to share her feelings. She tried to explain that although she enjoyed my company, she loved her work and the freedom it brought. Then gently she imparted the news that she had extended her contract in Saudi Arabia and would be returning there soon. Eunice's calling in Saudi was too strong for her to think of another kind of life, and I necessarily had to accept that call.

So the story was not to have the ultimate happy ending. But God has a calling for me, too. 'Help the disadvantaged,' he told me, and that is what I aim to do wherever he may lead me.

Perhaps one day God will also provide me with a wife with whom to share my life – or maybe he can use me more effectively as a single man helping his needy people. I have given my life into his service and I will submit gladly to his will, whatever it might be. I simply ask that he provide me with the grace to continue working for him through good times and bad.

It is particularly good that I am able to stay on the Isle of Man at this time so that I can be near my mother who is now alone since my father died. I frequently pop round to visit her and she sometimes looks back over the years when she struggled with the mountainous problem of a young baby born with no arms.

'Your father was distraught to begin with,' she recalls. 'It seemed impossible to manage with our other children being so young as well. We had no idea what we were going to do. We couldn't understand how you would get on without arms – we had to try to give you every opportunity to be "normal" by encouraging you to wear those awful false arms. But you soon showed us! Your feet and legs became your hands and arms from the day you reached out for your rattle! I'm glad your father lived to see you managing your life so well. You may be "wired to the moon", but he always had confidence that you would win in the end!'

I, too, remembered the days when all those around me seemed to think that life could not go on without arms. My thirteenth year proved momentous in two ways. First and most importantly, it was the year when I realised that God existed and that he loved me, personally. But even more, he loved me *as I was*. I did not need to have arms to be 'complete'. He had made me unique and special. He made me to live without arms. So significantly, my thirteenth year was the year I refused to wear arms any more. From that time on I could be myself; I could do the work God prepared for me to do; I could joyfully say, 'Look, Mum – no hands!'

Postscript

The death of my father in 1994 left a huge vacuum in the life of my mother. They had always been very close and she found it difficult to come to terms with the loss, and her health suffered. To add to her isolation, she did not see much of my sisters, Pat and Gwen, as they both had married and lived in England. Of course, I lived nearby and called in every day and my sisters wrote often, but we could not make up for the loss of Dad.

Therefore, in early March 1998, after much persuasion, Mum gathered enough strength to undertake the long journey to England to visit Pat and Gwen and their families. It was a wonderful holiday, but my sisters confided to me later that it seemed to them as though Mum was 'saying goodbye' . . .

She had only been home five weeks when she had another of her 'little turns'. 'I'm ready for the Lord to take me home,' she told me, but I laughed it off as after an hour's sleep she got up and spent Friday in her usual way – dusting and cleaning. At 10.15 p.m. that night she prepared for bed, tuning in to Manx Radio, whose programme of light music helped her to sleep.

Later that night I called in to make sure she was comfortable. I did not usually call in so late, but on this occasion I felt anxious. I found her peacefully in her bed, the radio still on, but Mum had had her final 'turn' – a heart attack which had taken her to be with the Lord Jesus.

As a Christian I rejoice that she is in a far better place with no more suffering, but as a man I miss her presence still. I could never repay her for her care and love that carried me through my darkest days. Suddenly my links with the past were severed, and I had to think about what I was going to do next.

I have always felt drawn to help people with disabilities but had no idea how to go about beginning such work. I prayed that God would show me what he wanted me to do. Then my colleagues, David Gordon and Gary Haire, suggested that I approach a Christian ministry for disabled people. I became aware of a newly established one with the unusual name 'Through the Roof'. This organisation is the UK disability outreach of an American woman, Joni Eareckson Tada, who as I mentioned in Chapter 14 was paralysed in a diving accident in 1967. She thought her life had ended because of almost total paralysis, but in rehabilitation found God gave her personal hope and purpose. She gradually developed talents which included preaching and teaching, singing, painting by mouth, and bringing vision and hope to disabled people, all of which have developed into a worldwide ministry. Having discovered that the organisation's aim to promote disability awareness reflected my own aspirations and passion, I joined 'Through the Roof' as a volunteer worker.

Yet the year 2000 turned out to be a very challenging, exciting and life-changing time and, after eighteen months with 'Through the Roof', I felt it was time to move on. Very special friends reminded me that faith is spelt 'R.I.S.K.' and that, rather than fearing failure, I should have faith that dreams from God come to pass. So after the privilege of serving Broadway Baptist Church full-time for eight years (a role which I juggled with my work for 'Through the Roof' for the last eighteen months), I'm now taking a wholehearted risk by launching a new ministry – 'Look, No Hands!' – which aims to reach children without limbs.

A verse in the Bible says 'God is able to do immeasurably more than all we ask or imagine, according to his power that is at work within us'. These words are on a beautiful linen banner hanging on a stone wall in my home church. They constantly remind me that together we can make a difference!

I believe that God will use my disability to help others come to faith in the God who never makes mistakes. He made me without arms for a purpose and I trust he will use me to take his love to those whom he has also created to be 'different'.

Surprise, surprise! On 25 August 2000, I got married to May in Randalstown, County Antrim. My heart had been stolen by a 'wee treasure' from Kells, County Antrim – only a dozen miles from Ballyclare, where I lived as a boy. I had known May for a few years here on the Isle of Man, as she had worked for a bank in Douglas and worshipped at Broadway. Then May was transferred back to her job in Belfast. During the summer of 1999 our friendship blossomed, and soon after Joni Eareckson Tada's visit to Belfast in early September, May and I knew deep in our hearts that God in his love had brought us together!

Appendix
The phoenix rises

The doctor was at a loss to know what to do. His patients suffered agonising pain through lesions caused by leprosy. Nothing seemed to help. In desperation he remembered that the infamous thalidomide had sedative properties. This was 1965 – just three years since the terrible consequences it had caused to pregnant women became known. Dare he try it again? But his patients were either men or women beyond child-bearing age. Surely it couldn't do them any harm? It was his only hope. At least it might relieve some of the pain.

When each of the patients returned excitedly a day or so after taking the drug, the doctor could hardly believe his eyes. The lesions had almost disappeared on all of them. Could it have been coincidence? The doctor questioned his patients closely. What else had they taken over the last few days? Where had they been? What had they been doing? The negative answers could mean only one thing: thalidomide had worked a miracle.

Since that remarkable discovery, thalidomide has begun to

make a comeback. Doctors have tried it for all manner of untreatable diseases, with amazing results in many cases. Leprosy is its most famous success, but it has prevented blindness in some countries and gone on to help patients with HIV and AIDS in Britain. In fact, some devotees are now hailing it as the wonder drug of all time.

Today it is not the huge disappointment and catastrophe that it represented in the early 1960s. It has re-emerged as a possible panacea for ills such as cancer, tuberculosis and rheumatoid arthritis, brain tumours, wasting and auto-immune diseases. It does not usually appear as 'thalidomide', however. It is manu-factured now under a variety of different names in the United States, Brazil, Britain and Canada; but in all the renewed hype, the dangers still remain.

Sadly, often where leprosy is worst, so is poverty and ignorance, and not all doctors are specific in warning about the risk to pregnant women. Instructions may be written on the bottle or box, but if one cannot read, what good is that? Then, where doctors are very careful to make the dangers known, who knows how many desperate people share or borrow another's medica-tion? In these circumstances, disasters happen.

The 'miracle' is becoming widely known. It is reported that thousands in South America are taking it for a terrible condition causing extreme ulceration of the mouth, but also for stomach disorders and even to help skin grafts. It would seem that there is no end to the miracles performed by thalidomide, but clearly there has to be some legislation with regard to its use in order to avoid a recurrence of the catastrophic results experienced in the 1960s when around twelve thousand children were born with missing limbs.

The United States, however, suffered less from babies without limbs because of the suspicions of a far-sighted specialist. Since thalidomide began to re-emerge from its disgrace, it has been used in the States with the utmost care, only now treating many patients each year who could otherwise not be helped. But to prescribe it, all those concerned must abide by strict rules. Doctors, chemists and pharmacists can only acquire it if they have been properly trained regarding the dangers and, together with the patient, they must be enrolled in a government-monitored registry. If it is to be prescribed to women of child-bearing age, then those women are instructed to use birth control methods while they are taking thalidomide, and have to sign a document to that effect.

All this is commonsense management, but seems to be only happening in the United States. Other countries are either not so particular or haven't the resources to put such a scheme in place. It would, indeed, seem that thalidomide can help many suffering people; and who would deny their hope of recovery? But something must be done to avoid the disaster of past years.

Brazil is well known to have children still being born with deformities. Most of them will have no access to the assistance given to thalidomide victims in Britain or America. These children remain in poverty and ignorance, many with no hope of ever earning a reasonable living.

It is hoped that this book will go some way to helping those children in particular, which is why I have decided to donate my royalties from the sales to help ease their suffering and raise awareness of their plight.

Look, No Hands!
All correspondence and donations should be sent to the office below:

Look, No Hands!
The Alpha Centre
Broadway
Douglas
Isle of Man
IM2 4EN
British Isles

Web site: www.looknohands.org

Isle of Man Registered Charity No. 762